D0777051

ORGANIZED TO DO JEHOVAH'S WILL

"To do your will,
O my God, I have delighted."
—Ps. 40:8.

This Book Issued To ____________________

Date ____________

Place of Baptism ____________________

Date ____________

Publishers
Watchtower Bible and Tract Society of New York, Inc.
Brooklyn, New York, U.S.A.

Unless otherwise indicated, Scripture quotations
are from the modern-language
*New World Translation of the Holy Scriptures
—With References*

Organized to Do Jehovah's Will
English (*od*-E)

Made in the United States of America

CONTENTS

Dear Fellow Ministers:

Organized to Do Jehovah's Will is published for Jehovah's Witnesses. This book makes clear what is involved in pleasing God and finding delight in doing his will. It provides an overall view of how the Christian congregation is organized for getting God's work done. The book offers counsel and direction to help us maintain unity with our brothers worldwide. (1 Pet. 2:17; 5:9) It highlights how we can have a share in declaring the good news of the Kingdom in recognition of God's will that "all sorts of men . . . come to an accurate knowledge of truth."—1 Tim. 2:4; Matt. 24:14.

In addition to preaching the good news of the Kingdom, we desire to render needed spiritual assistance to all those who are being drawn to Jehovah in response to the invitation to praise him in association with his people. (Ps. 145:21; Rev. 22:17) New ones need to become familiar with the operation of Jehovah's organization and learn how they can have a share in the modern-day preaching work. They are encouraged to continue in their endeavors to meet the Scriptural requirements for becoming dedicated and baptized Witnesses of Jehovah.

General information is here published concerning the duties of elders and ministerial servants, judicial procedures, and various other features of congregation organization. Details regarding these matters are reviewed from time to time in *The Watchtower, Our Kingdom Ministry,* and other publications of Jehovah's Witnesses.

It is our prayer that the application of what is contained in this publication will help you to progress spiritually. May you continue to find delight in doing Jehovah's will in harmony with his organized people!

Governing Body of Jehovah's Witnesses

CHAPTER 1

ORGANIZED TO DO JEHOVAH'S WILL

THROUGHOUT the world, there are thousands of national and international organizations. Among them are a host of religious, political, commercial, and social organizations with varying characteristics and objectives. Their memberships, large and small, are organized according to human viewpoints and philosophies. But there is one organization that is outstandingly different from all the rest. God's Word along with abundant well-documented evidence clearly identifies that organization as none other than Jehovah's Witnesses.

Happily, as one of Jehovah's dedicated, baptized Witnesses, you are now associated with Jehovah's organization. Having proved to yourself what God's will is, you are now doing it. (Ps. 143:10; Rom. 12:2) You are an active minister serving with a loving, worldwide association of brothers. (2 Cor. 6:4; 1 Pet. 2:17; 5:9) As Jesus promised, this brings you rich blessings in this period of time. (Prov. 10:22; Mark 10:30) By faithfully and unitedly doing Jehovah's will, you are being prepared for a lasting, glorious future. —1 Tim. 6:18, 19; 1 John 2:17.

How faith strengthening and beneficial it is that our Grand Creator has a unique and wonderful worldwide organization that is theocratic! This means that it is ruled by Jehovah as Head over all. We have complete confidence in him. He is our Judge, Lawgiver, and eternal King. (Isa. 33:22) Being a God of order, he has coordinated arrangements for our working harmoniously with him in serving the divine purpose. —2 Cor. 6:1, 2.

As the end of the present system of things draws ever nearer, we move ahead loyally and obediently under the leadership of our appointed Commander and Messianic King, Christ Jesus. (Isa. 55:4; Rev. 6:2; 11:15) It was none other than Jesus who foretold that his followers would do works greater than those he accomplished during his earthly ministry of Kingdom preaching and disciple making. (John 14: 12) That would be so because over a longer period of time and in increasing numbers, Jesus' followers would cover a widening territory. They would proclaim the Kingdom good news to the extremities of the earth and make disciples of people of all the nations.—Matt. 24:14; 28:19, 20; Acts 1:8.

This has already proved to be a reality, as has been progressively documented in *Yearbooks of Jehovah's Witnesses*. However, as Jesus clearly stated, the activity of declaring the good news of divine judgment will end at Jehovah's appointed time. All indications of God's prophetic Word point to Jehovah's great and fear-inspiring day as having drawn close.—Zeph. 1: 14-18; 2:2, 3; 1 Pet. 4:7.

Perceiving what the will of Jehovah is at this late hour, his organization is imbued with a sense of urgency. There is a need to intensify our efforts in doing what God requires. This calls for us to become well acquainted with the way God's organization functions and to cooperate fully with it. The operation of the organization is based on Scriptural principles, including the commandments, laws, orders, regulations, and teachings set out in God's inspired Word.—Ps. 19:7-9.

By observing and adhering to such Bible-based direction, all of Jehovah's people dwell and work together in peace and unity. (Ps. 133:1; Isa. 60:17;

Rom. 14:19) What strengthens bonds among our brothers everywhere? It is the fact that we are motivated by and clothed with love. (John 13:34, 35; Col. 3:14) In this divinely favored way, we keep pace with the heavenly part of Jehovah's organization.

THE HEAVENLY PART OF JEHOVAH'S ORGANIZATION

The prophets Isaiah, Daniel, and Ezekiel saw visions of the heavenly part of Jehovah's organization. (Isa., chap. 6; Ezek., chap. 1; Dan. 7:9, 10) Likewise, the apostle John had a vision of this heavenly arrangement and afforded us a glimpse of it in the book of Revelation. He saw Jehovah on a glorious throne accompanied by angelic creatures who proclaim: "Holy, holy, holy is Jehovah God, the Almighty, who was and who is and who is coming." (Rev. 4:8) John also saw "standing in the midst of the throne . . . a lamb." It is the Lamb of God, Jesus Christ.—Rev. 5:6, 13, 14; John 1:29.

John's vision means that at the head of the heavenly part of Jehovah's organization is Jehovah God on his throne. Regarding him and his superior position, 1 Chronicles 29:11, 12 states: "Yours, O Jehovah, are the greatness and the mightiness and the beauty and the excellency and the dignity; for everything in the heavens and in the earth is yours. Yours is the kingdom, O Jehovah, the One also lifting yourself up as head over all. The riches and the glory are on account of you, and you are dominating everything; and in your hand there are power and mightiness, and in your hand is ability to make great and to give strength to all."

As Jehovah's fellow worker, Jesus Christ occupies an elevated position in the heavens, and much authority has been delegated to him. Indeed, God "subjected all things under his feet, and made him head over all things to the congregation." (Eph. 1:22) The apostle Paul said of Jesus: "God exalted him to a superior position and kindly gave him the name that is above every other name, so that in the name of Jesus every knee should bend of those in heaven and those on earth and those under the ground, and every tongue should openly acknowledge that Jesus Christ is Lord to the glory of God the Father." (Phil. 2:9-11) Thus, we can have full confidence in the righteous leadership of Jesus Christ.

The prophet Daniel saw in vision the Ancient of Days on His throne and angels numbering "a thousand thousands that kept ministering to him, and ten thousand times ten thousand that kept standing right before him." (Dan. 7:10) The Bible refers to this heavenly army of angels as "spirits for public service, sent forth to minister for those who are going to inherit salvation." (Heb. 1:14) All these spirit creatures are organized into 'thrones, lordships, governments, and authorities.'—Col. 1:16.

When we take time to contemplate these features of the heavenly part of Jehovah's organization, we can understand Isaiah's reaction to the vision in which he "got to see Jehovah, sitting on a throne," and "seraphs were standing above him." Isaiah stated: "Woe to me! For I am as good as brought to silence, because a man unclean in lips I am, and in among a people unclean in lips I am dwelling; for my eyes have seen the King, Jehovah of armies, himself!" Indeed, Isaiah was awestruck and humbled when he grasped the scope of Jehovah's organization. He was so deeply affected by this experience that when a call went out from heaven regarding a special work of proclaiming Jehovah's judgments, Isaiah's reaction was: "Here I am! Send me."—Isa. 6: 1-5, 8.

Recognizing and appreciating Jehovah's organization motivates his people in a similar way. As the organization moves forward, we willingly and zealously endeavor to keep up with it. We strive to demonstrate our confidence in Jehovah's organization today.

JEHOVAH'S ORGANIZATION ON THE MOVE

In chapter 1 of Ezekiel's prophecy, Jehovah is pictured as riding on a colossal celestial chariot. This resplendent vehicle pictures the invisible part of Jehovah's organization. He rides this chariot in the sense of benevolently dominating it and using it according to his purpose.—Ps. 103:20.

Each wheel of this chariot has a wheel inside it—one of the same diameter that fits crosswise into the base wheel. Only in this way can the wheels be said to "go on their four respective sides." (Ezek. 1: 17) The wheels can instantly change direction because there is a side of the wheel facing in each direction. However, this chariot is not without control or intelligent supervision. Jehovah does not let his organization go in any direction that it might be inclined to go. Ezekiel 1:20 says: "Wherever the spirit inclined to go, they would go." Thus, it is Jehovah who causes his organization to move to wherever his spirit impels it to move. The question we must ask ourselves is, 'Am I in step with it?'

Keeping pace with Jehovah's organization involves more than just attending meetings and participating in the field ministry. Primarily, our keeping pace has to do with progress and spiritual growth. It involves 'making sure of the more important things' and staying up-to-date with the spiritual feeding program. (Phil. 1:10; 4:8, 9; John 17:3) We must remember, too, that where there is organization, there is a need for good coordination and cooperation. So we must be alert to the importance of making the best use of the spiritual and material assets that Jehovah has entrusted to us in order to accomplish his work. As we keep pace with Jehovah's celestial chariot, our lives are consistent with the message we proclaim.

With the help of Jehovah's organization, we are all moving forward in doing God's will. Remember that the Rider of this celestial chariot is Jehovah. Therefore, keeping pace with the heavenly chariot shows that we have respect for Jehovah and confidence in our "rock." (Ps. 18:31) The Bible promises: "Jehovah himself will give strength indeed to his people. Jehovah himself will bless his people with peace." (Ps. 29:11) Being a part of Jehovah's organization today, we share in the strength that he gives and enjoy the peace with which he blesses his organized people. Yes, there is no question about it, rich blessings will continue to be ours as we do Jehovah's will now and forever.

CHAPTER 2

RECOGNIZING CHRIST'S ROLE IN GOD'S ARRANGEMENT

"IN THE beginning God created the heavens and the earth," and everything he made was "very good." (Gen. 1:1, 31) Jehovah made man with wonderful prospects for the future. However, the rebellion in Eden temporarily interrupted mankind's happy state. Yet, Jehovah's purpose for the earth and for mankind remained unchanged. Even in pronouncing sentence upon those who had rebelled against his sovereignty, God indicated that there would be deliverance for obedient descendants of Adam. There would be a restoration of true worship, and God would destroy the wicked one together with all his evil works. (Gen. 3:15) Once again things will be "very good." Jehovah will accomplish this through his Son, Jesus Christ. (1 John 3:8) Therefore, it is imperative that we recognize Christ's role in God's arrangement.—Acts 4:12; Phil. 2:9, 11.

WHAT CHRIST'S ROLE IS

When thinking of Christ's role in God's arrangement, we must recognize that his role has many facets. Jesus serves as mankind's Redeemer, as High Priest, as Head of the Christian congregation, and now as King of God's Kingdom. Meditating on these roles heightens our appreciation for God's arrangement and deepens our love for Christ Jesus. The Bible describes his varied roles.

During Christ's earthly ministry, it became clear that the reconciliation of obedient mankind to God would be accomplished through Jesus. (John 14:6) As mankind's Redeemer, he gave himself as a ransom in exchange for many. (Matt. 20:28) So Jesus served as more than just an example of godly conduct. He became the key figure in the outworking of Jehovah's purpose for mankind. He is our only means of being restored to God's favor. (Acts 5:31; 2 Cor. 5:18, 19) Jesus' sacrificial death and his resurrection have opened the way for obedient mankind to experience eternal blessings under the rule of God's heavenly Kingdom.

From his heavenly position, Jesus Christ also serves as High Priest. As such, he is able to "sympathize with our weaknesses" and make atonement for the sins of his dedicated followers here on earth. The apostle Paul explained: "We have as high priest, not one who cannot sympathize with our weaknesses, but one who has been tested in all respects like ourselves, but without sin." Paul then encourages those who exercise faith in Jesus Christ to take full advantage of this arrangement for reconciliation to God, saying: "Let us, therefore, approach with freeness of speech to the throne of undeserved kindness . . . for help at the right time."—Heb. 4:14-16; 1 John 2:2.

Jesus also lovingly serves as Head of the Christian congregation. Just as was true of his followers in the first century, so we today have no need of a human leader. Jesus gives direction through holy spirit, through the Holy Scriptures, and through qualified undershepherds, who are accountable to him and to his heavenly Father as they care for the flock of God. (Heb. 13:17; 1 Pet. 5:2, 3) Speaking prophetically of Jesus, Jehovah said: "Look! As a witness to the national groups I have given him, as a leader and commander to the national groups." (Isa. 55:4) Jesus confirmed the fulfillment of this prophecy in himself when he told his disciples: "Neither be called 'leaders,' for your Leader is one, the Christ."—Matt. 23:10.

As an expression of his mental attitude and willingness to help us, Jesus extends the invitation: "Come to me, all you who are toiling and loaded down, and I will refresh you. Take my yoke upon you and learn from me, for I am mild-tempered and lowly in heart, and you will find refreshment for your souls. For my yoke is kindly and my load is light." (Matt. 11:28-30) By administering the affairs of the Christian congregation with mildness and in a way that brings refreshment to our souls, Jesus Christ has proved himself to be "the fine shepherd" in imitation of his heavenly Father, Jehovah God.—John 10:11; Isa. 40:11.

In his first letter to the Corinthians, Paul explained another facet of Jesus Christ's role, in these words: "He must rule as king until God has put all enemies under his feet. But when all things will have been subjected to him, then the Son himself will also subject himself to the One who subjected all things to him, that God may be all things to everyone." (1 Cor. 15:25, 28) Before coming to earth, Jesus served in heaven as God's "master worker," being the first of God's creations. (Prov. 8:22-31) When God sent Jesus to earth, he did God's will at all times. He endured the supreme test and died faithful to his Father. (John 4:34; 15:10) For his loyalty to God even to death, Jesus was rewarded. God resurrected him to heaven and gave him the right to be King of the heavenly Kingdom. (Acts 2:32-36) As King of the Kingdom, Christ Jesus has the awesome assignment from God to lead myriads of powerful spirit creatures in removing human rule from the earth and ridding our globe of all wickedness. (Prov. 2:21, 22; 2 Thess. 1:6-9; Rev. 19:11-21; 20:1-3) Then God's heavenly Kingdom under Christ will be the only ruling authority over the entire earth.—Rev. 11:15.

WHAT RECOGNITION OF HIS ROLE MEANS

Jesus Christ, our Exemplar, is perfect. He has been commissioned to care for us. Jehovah God has entrusted Jesus Christ with the serious responsibility of being Leader and Commander of God's people today. Therefore, recognition of Christ's role in God's arrangement means that we remain loyal to Jehovah and keep in step with his progressive organization.

Jesus' followers in the first century fully recognized the role of Christ in God's arrangement. They showed this by working together in unity under the headship of Christ, submitting themselves to his direction given by means of holy spirit and the inspired Scriptures. (Acts 15:12-21; Rev. 1:1) The apostle Paul made reference to the unity of the anointed Christian congregation when he wrote: "Speaking the truth, let us by love grow up in all things into him who is the head, Christ. From him all the body, by being harmoniously joined together and being made to cooperate through every joint that gives what is needed, according to the functioning of each respective member in due measure, makes for the growth of the body for the building up of itself in love." —Eph. 4:15, 16.

Like the human body, the congregation of anointed ones and "other sheep" is made up of many different members. When each member of the congregation cooperates with the others and all work in harmony under Christ's headship, there is growth and we maintain a warm spirit of love, which is "a perfect bond of union."—John 10:16; Col. 3:14; 1 Cor. 12:14-26.

World events fulfilling Bible prophecy prove beyond doubt that since 1914, Jesus Christ has been entrusted with Kingdom power. He is now ruling in the midst of his enemies. (Ps. 2:1-12; 110:1, 2) What does this signify for those now living on earth? As for his enemies, Jesus will powerfully demonstrate his role as King of kings and Lord of lords when he executes divine judgment against them. (Rev. 11:15; 12:10; 19:16) Jehovah's promise of deliverance expressed at the beginning of man's rebellion will soon be fulfilled toward those at His right hand of favor. (Rom. 16:20) How happy we are to have recognized Christ's role in God's arrangement and to be unified to accomplish a worldwide ministry under Christ's leadership during these last days!

CHAPTER 3

TRUSTING "THE FAITHFUL AND DISCREET SLAVE"

"WHO really is the faithful and discreet slave?" With that question, Jesus Christ introduced a parable, or illustration, of prophetic importance. It is part of "the sign" he gave regarding "the conclusion of the system of things." (Matt. 24:3, 42-47) Jesus indicated that the "slave" would be busy during the time of the end. "That slave" would be entrusted with oversight of Kingdom interests on earth and have the serious responsibility of providing God's people with spiritual food "at the proper time." In this connection Jesus further stated: "Happy is that slave if his master on arriving finds him doing so. Truly I say to you, He will appoint him over all his belongings."

This parable raises serious questions for our consideration. Who is "that slave"? What are the "belongings"? What part do we individually play in this prophetic illustration? Such questions are not of mere academic interest. Properly identifying these things and maintaining trust in "the faithful and discreet slave" helps us to do Jehovah's will.

IDENTIFYING "THE FAITHFUL AND DISCREET SLAVE"

In the illustration, Jesus stated that the "slave" would provide the needed spiritual food. Whom did Jesus appoint to feed his followers in the first century? And whom did he find still faithfully doing so when he returned in Kingdom power in 1914? Obviously, no human has lived through all those centuries. So "the faithful steward, the discreet one," must symbolize the composite body of Christ's spirit-anointed footstep followers who live on earth at any given time. (Luke 12:42) Yes, Christ uses this body to publish information on the fulfillment of Bible prophecies and to give timely direction on the application of Bible principles in daily life. In turn, this spiritual food is distributed through the local congregations of Jehovah's Witnesses.—Isa. 43:10; Gal. 6:16.

What, then, are the "belongings"? These are all the spiritual assets on earth that have become Christ's property in connection with his authority as heavenly King. Included are facilities at the headquarters of Jehovah's Witnesses, along with branch offices, Kingdom Halls, and Assembly Halls worldwide. The "belongings" also embrace the commission to preach "this good news of the kingdom" throughout the earth and to teach those who respond. The "slave" serves as God's instrument to gather into association with the congregation "a great crowd . . . out of all nations and tribes and peoples and tongues," who will survive the great tribulation. (Luke 12:42-44; Matt. 24:14; Rev. 7:9-14) In fact, this great crowd plays a large part in seeing to it that the good news is preached to the ends of the earth. They are among the precious "belongings" of Christ and are greatly loved by the slave class for their loyal, zealous support.

THE ROLE OF THE GOVERNING BODY

"The faithful and discreet slave" seeks to preserve unity and makes it possible organizationally for 'all things to take place decently and by arrangement.' (1 Cor. 14:40) To accomplish this in the first century, a group of anointed Christians from among the faithful and discreet slave class were chosen as its representatives. As such, they did not consult with all anointed elders in the world before making decisions. From their position in the Jerusalem congregation, they served as a governing body for the entire anointed Christian congregation.

From Pentecost 33 C.E. onward, the faithful apostles of the Lord Jesus Christ took the lead in providing direction for the newly founded Christian congregation. (Acts 4:33, 35, 37; 5:18, 29) By about the year 49 C.E., this governing body had been enlarged to include more than Jesus' apostles. When the circumcision issue was decided, that body included "the apostles and older men in Jerusalem." (Acts 15:1, 2) It was their responsibility to consider matters affecting Christians everywhere. They sent out letters and decrees, all of which strengthened the congregations and made it possible for the disciples to remain united in thought and action. The congregations followed the direction of the governing body, and as a result, they received Jehovah's blessing and prospered.—Acts 8:1, 14, 15; 15:22-31; 16:4, 5.

The value of such an arrangement is evident today. The anointed ones making up the present-day Governing Body of Jehovah's Witnesses have decades of faithful service and theocratic experience behind them. They offer spiritual direction to Jehovah's people, as did the first-century governing body. The Governing Body also continues to carry the responsibility of overseeing the preaching work, producing Bible study material, and arranging for the appointment of overseers to serve in various capacities in the organization. These are some of the Kingdom interests of Christ that are being cared for today. Like the early Christians, we gladly look to spiritually mature men for Bible-based direction and guidance in matters of worship.

As was true in the first century, the Governing Body today is made up of imperfect men. However, Jehovah has used imperfect humans in the past to accomplish his will. He instructed Noah to build an ark and to preach about the coming destruction of his day. (Gen. 6:13, 14, 22; 2 Pet. 2:5) Moses was appointed to lead Jehovah's people out of Egypt. (Ex. 3:10) Imperfect men were inspired to write the Bible. (2 Tim. 3:16; 2 Pet. 1:21) Jehovah's use of imperfect men today to direct the preaching and disciple-making work does not weaken our confidence in God's organization. Rather, we are strengthened because we know that without Jehovah's backing, the Governing Body could never accomplish all that they do.

WHY TRUST "THE FAITHFUL AND DISCREET SLAVE"

There are many reasons to have complete trust in the slave class. First and foremost, Jesus has appointed them over *all* his precious "belongings." This is a clear indication that he has complete trust in them.

Second, God's Word admonishes Christians to cooperate fully with those taking the lead. Why is this to our advantage? As recorded at Hebrews 13:17, the apostle Paul stated: "Be obedient to those who are taking the lead among you and be submissive, for they are keeping watch over your souls as those who will render an account; that they may do this with joy and not with sighing, for this would be damaging to you." For our spiritual protection and well-being, it is incumbent upon us to be obedient and submissive to direction from overseers as they 'keep watch over our souls.'

As recorded at 1 Corinthians 16:14, Paul stated: "Let all your affairs take place with love." Decisions made in behalf of God's people are influenced by this superior quality of love. Regarding love, 1 Corinthians 13:4-8 states: "Love is long-suffering and kind. Love is not jealous, it does not brag, does not get puffed up, does not behave indecently, does not look for its own interests, does not become provoked. It does not keep account of the injury. It does not rejoice over unrighteousness, but rejoices with the truth. It bears all things, believes all things, hopes all things, endures all things. Love never fails." Since love dominates all of the decisions that are made for the benefit of Jehovah's servants, we have every reason to feel secure under such direction. Moreover, this is simply a reflection of Jehovah's love for all his people.

Through much hardship and experience, the slave class has demonstrated that the spirit of God is with it. Abundant blessings have been poured out upon the visible part of Jehovah's organization today, and therefore, we wholeheartedly give it our full support and trust.

HOW WE DEMONSTRATE OUR TRUST

Those who are appointed to responsible positions in the congregation demonstrate their trust by gladly accepting and faithfully discharging the obligations of their appointments. (Acts 20:28) As Kingdom proclaimers, we zealously engage in the house-to-house work, make return visits, and conduct home Bible studies. (Matt. 24:14; 28:19, 20) In order to benefit fully from the rich spiritual food being dispensed by "the faithful and discreet slave," we prepare well for and attend all our Christian meetings. This includes assemblies and conventions that are arranged each year. We greatly benefit from the interchange of encouragement that takes place when freely associating with our brothers at these Christian gatherings. —Heb. 10:24, 25.

Our trust in 'the faithful slave' is also manifest when we support the organization with our material contributions. (Prov. 3:9, 10) When we see that our brothers are in need materially, we respond without delay. (Gal. 6:10; 1 Tim. 6:18) This we do in a real spirit of brotherly love, constantly being on the alert for opportunities to show our appreciation to Jehovah and his organization for the goodness bestowed upon us.—John 13:35.

Another way to show that we trust the slave class today is to support its decisions. Even though we may not fully understand the reasoning behind certain decisions, we know that upholding them will be for our lasting good. On occasion important issues have been clarified, and we have wholeheartedly supported these decisions. As a result, Jehovah blesses us for our obedience to his Word and to the slave class. We thus show our subjection to the Master, Jesus Christ.

Yes, we have every reason to trust "the faithful and discreet slave" fully. Satan, the god of this system of things, is making an all-out effort to disgrace Jehovah's name and organization. (2 Cor. 4:4) Do not fall prey to Satan's wicked tactics. (2 Cor. 2:11) He knows that only a short period of time remains before his abyssing, and he is trying to take down with him as many of Jehovah's people as possible. (Rev. 12:12) However, as Satan intensifies his efforts, may we draw ever closer to Jehovah by manifesting complete trust in the channel that He is using to direct His people today. Satan is waging war against "the remaining ones" of the slave class, who have been entrusted with directing "the work of bearing witness to Jesus." (Rev. 12:17) Our full confidence in Jehovah and his arrangements results in a united brotherhood.

CHAPTER 4

HOW THE CONGREGATION IS ORGANIZED AND GOVERNED

THE apostle Paul in his first letter to the Corinthians expressed an important truth about God when he wrote: "God is a God, not of disorder, but of peace." Then commenting further with regard to congregation meetings, he said: "Let all things take place decently and by arrangement."—1 Cor. 14: 33, 40.

At the very beginning of the same letter, the apostle gave admonition concerning reported dissensions within the Corinthian congregation. Paul exhorted the brothers there to "speak in agreement" and to be "fitly united in the same mind and in the same line of thought." (1 Cor. 1:10, 11) He then gave counsel with regard to various matters that were affecting the unity of the congregation. Using the illustration of a human body, he showed clearly the need for unity and cooperation. Hence, he urged all in the Christian congregation, regardless of their role, to care for one another in a loving way. (1 Cor. 12:12-26) Such harmonious cooperation among the members of the congregation implies an orderly arrangement—organization.

But how was the Christian congregation to be organized? Who would organize it? What kind of structure would it have, and who would serve in appointed positions? By letting the Bible be our guide, we get clear answers to these questions.—1 Cor. 4:6.

ORGANIZED THEOCRATICALLY

The Christian congregation was established in 33 C.E. on the Jewish festival day of Pentecost. What can we learn about the congregation at that time? It was organized and governed theocratically, that is, under God (Greek, *the·os'*) rule (*kra'tos*). The inspired account of what took place there in Jerusalem nearly 2,000 years ago leaves no doubt that the congregation of anointed Christians was established by God. (Acts 2:1-47) It was his building, his household. (1 Cor. 3:9; Eph. 2:19) The same pattern of organization and operation that was established during the first century is adhered to by the Christian congregation of God today, which has now been enlarged by the addition of the "great crowd."—Rev. 7:9, 10.

The early congregation began with about 120 members. Holy spirit was poured out first upon these in fulfillment of Joel 2:28, 29. (Acts 2:16-18) But that same day, about 3,000 others were baptized in water and brought into the spirit-begotten congregation. They had embraced the word about the Christ and "continued devoting themselves to the teaching of the apostles." After that, "Jehovah continued to join to them daily those being saved."—Acts 2:41, 42, 47.

The growth of the anointed congregation in Jerusalem became such that the Jewish high priest complained that the disciples had filled Jerusalem with their teaching. The new disciples in Jerusalem included many Jewish priests, who became part of the congregation.—Acts 5:28; 6:7.

Jesus had said: "You will be witnesses of me both in Jerusalem and in all Judea and Samaria and to the most distant part of the earth." (Acts 1:8) And so it was that when great persecution arose in Jerusalem following the death of Stephen, the disciples living there were scattered throughout Judea and Samaria. But wherever they went, they continued declaring the good news and making more disciples, including some from among the Samaritans. (Acts 8:1-13) Still later, the good news began to be preached with good success among the uncircumcised, non-Jewish nations. (Acts 10:1-48) All this preaching activity and the making of many disciples resulted in new Christian congregations being formed outside Jerusalem. —Acts 11:19-21; 14:21-23.

What arrangements were made to ensure that each newly established congregation was organized and governed God's way, theocratically? Through the operation of God's spirit, provision was made for undershepherds to care for the flock. In congregations that Paul and Barnabas visited during their first missionary journey, they made appointments of older men. (Acts 14:23) Acts chapter 20 relates information about the apostle Paul's meeting with the older men of the congregation in Ephesus. Paul said to them: "Pay attention to yourselves and to all the flock, among which the holy spirit has appointed you overseers, to shepherd the congregation of God, which he purchased with the blood of his own Son." (Acts 20:28) These were older men in a spiritual sense. They qualified for appointment because of meeting Scriptural requirements. (1 Tim. 3:1-7) Paul's fellow worker Titus was authorized to make appointments of older men in the congregations of Crete.—Titus 1:5.

As more congregations were formed, the apostles and older men in Jerusalem continued to serve as the principal overseers of the expanded international congregation of the first century. They served as a governing body for the entire Christian congregation.

Writing to the congregation in Ephesus, the apostle Paul explained that by working in accord with God's spirit, the Christian congregation could maintain unity through adherence to the headship of Jesus Christ. The apostle urged Christians there to cultivate humility and to observe the oneness of the spirit in peaceful association with all members of the congregation. (Eph. 4:1-6) Then he quoted Psalm 68:18 and applied it to Jehovah's provision for spiritually qualified men to serve the needs of the congregation as apostles, prophets, evangelizers, shepherds, and teachers. Such men, as gifts from Jehovah, would build up the entire congregation to a spiritual fullness that would be pleasing to God.—Eph. 4:7-16.

CONGREGATION TODAY FOLLOWS APOSTOLIC PATTERN

Today a similar pattern of organization is followed in all congregations of Jehovah's Witnesses. These collectively form a united worldwide congregation built around the nucleus of spirit-anointed ones. (Zech. 8:23) This is possible because Jesus Christ, true to his promise, has loyally remained with his anointed disciples "all the days until the conclusion of the system of things." Those brought into the growing congregation today embrace the good news of God, dedicate their life unreservedly to Jehovah God to do his will, and are baptized as disciples of Jesus Christ. (Matt. 28:19, 20; Mark 1:14; Acts 2:41) They recognize "the fine shepherd," Jesus Christ, as Head not only over the anointed members of the congregation but also over the entire flock, which includes the "other sheep." (John 10:14, 16; Eph. 1:22, 23) That "one flock" maintain their unity by loyally recognizing the headship of Christ and also by submitting to the organizational channel, "the faithful and discreet slave," whom Christ appointed. May we continue to manifest full confidence and trust in this faithful slave class today.—Matt. 24:45.

USE OF RELIGIOUS CORPORATIONS

During these last days of this wicked system of things, the belongings of the Master have increased abundantly throughout all the earth. This has placed a heavy responsibility on 'the faithful slave.' In discharging the responsibility to provide spiritual food at the proper time and in order to get the good news of the Kingdom preached before the end comes, the slave class has formed certain agencies, or legal entities. It has proved to be the course of wisdom to organize certain corporations that are recognized by the laws of various countries. These religious corporations own and operate printing facilities that produce and distribute Bibles and Bible literature worldwide for use in the Kingdom ministry.

These corporations are exclusively devoted to advancing the interests of true worship in the earth. All these legal instrumentalities cooperate with one another. Such legal corporations are used to facilitate the preaching of the good news worldwide and to care for the spiritual needs of the entire congregation of God in all parts of the earth.

STRUCTURE OF BRANCH ORGANIZATION

Whenever a branch office is established, a Branch Committee of three or more elders is appointed to care for the various responsibilities involved in looking after the work in the country or countries under the jurisdiction of that particular branch. One member of the committee serves as the Branch Committee coordinator.

Local congregations under each branch are organized into circuits, and a number of circuits make up a district. Circuits and districts may be of various sizes, depending on geographic and language considerations as well as the number of congregations within the area assigned to the branch. A circuit overseer is appointed to serve the congregations in each circuit. A district overseer visits the different circuits, serves at circuit assemblies, and spends some time serving congregations, usually with the circuit overseer present. The duties of traveling overseers are set out from time to time in *Our Kingdom Ministry* as well as in correspondence directed to them by the branch office.

All in the organization recognize God's administration. The congregations acknowledge and conform to organizational arrangements that are outlined for the benefit of all. They accept the appointment of older men who oversee the work in branches, districts, circuits, and congregations. They look to "the faithful and discreet slave" for spiritual food at the proper time. 'The faithful slave' today, in turn, adheres strictly to the headship of Christ, holds to Bible principles, and submits to the direction of the holy spirit. As all work together in unity, they experience results similar to those experienced by the congregations in the first century. We are told at Acts 16:5: "Indeed, the congregations continued to be made firm in the faith and to increase in number from day to day."

CHAPTER 5

OVERSEERS TO SHEPHERD THE FLOCK

DURING his earthly ministry, Jesus proved himself to be "the fine shepherd." (John 10:11) Upon viewing the crowds that eagerly followed him, "he felt pity for them, because they were skinned and thrown about like sheep without a shepherd." (Matt. 9:36) Peter and the other apostles took note of his loving concern. How different Jesus was from the false shepherds of Israel, who neglected the flock to such an extent that the sheep were scattered and spiritually starved! (Ezek. 34:7, 8) By paying attention to Jesus' fine example of teaching and to the way he cared for the sheep even to the point of laying down his life for them, the apostles learned how to help those with faith return to Jehovah, 'the shepherd and overseer of their souls.'—1 Pet. 2:25.

By precept and example, Jesus emphasized the serious responsibility that he laid upon the apostles to care for the sheep. When speaking to Peter on one occasion, Jesus impressed very strongly upon the minds and hearts of the apostles the importance of feeding and shepherding the sheep. (John 21:15-17) Peter was deeply moved by this, as indicated later in his exhortation to older men. In his first inspired letter, he admonished overseers: "Shepherd the flock of God in your care, not under compulsion, but willingly; neither for love of dishonest gain, but eagerly; neither as lording it over those who are God's inheritance, but becoming examples to the flock."—1 Pet. 5:1-3.

Peter's words apply with equal force to overseers in the congregation today. The responsibility of overseers today is the same as it was in the first century, namely, to shepherd the flock of God. In his letter, Peter emphasized the proper attitude that overseers should have in caring for such responsibility. Imitating Jesus, they should serve willingly and eagerly as examples to the flock, taking the lead in Jehovah's service.

We can be grateful for the spirit-appointed overseers in the congregation. The benefits we receive are many. For example, overseers give spiritual encouragement and personal attention to the needs of individual members of the congregation. Each week they preside with earnestness at congregation meetings, where all are nourished in the faith. (Rom. 12:8) Their efforts to protect the flock from harmful elements, such as wicked men, contribute to our spiritual security. (Isa. 32:2; Titus 1:9-11) Their fine example and lead in the field ministry encourage us to keep active in preaching the good news regularly each month. (Phil. 3:16, 17; Heb. 13:15-17) Through these "gifts in men," Jehovah has provided well for the building up of the congregation.—Eph. 4:8, 11, 12.

QUALIFICATIONS FOR OVERSEERS

To ensure proper care of the congregation, men appointed to serve as overseers must meet the requirements set out in God's Word. Only if they qualify can it be said that they are appointed by holy spirit. (Acts 20:28) Admittedly, the Scriptural standards for Christian overseers are high, since these men have the serious responsibilities of taking the lead in Jehovah's worship and of being exemplary in Christian conduct. (1 Cor. 11:1; Heb. 13:7) But the standards are not so high that they cannot be met by Christian men who have real love for Jehovah and are willing to be used by him. The high standards call for those appointed as elders to be good examples in the congregation. It should be obvious to all that the overseers are individuals who apply Bible counsel in the affairs of life.

The apostle Paul set out in his first letter to Timothy and his letter to Titus the basic Scriptural requirements for overseers. At 1 Timothy 3:1-7, we read: "If any man is reaching out for an office of overseer, he is desirous of a fine work. The overseer should therefore be irreprehensible, a husband of one wife, moderate in habits, sound in mind, orderly, hospitable, qualified to teach, not a drunken brawler, not a smiter, but reasonable, not belligerent, not a lover of money, a man presiding over his own household in a fine manner, having children in subjection with all seriousness; (if indeed any man does not know how to preside over his own household, how will he take care of God's congregation?) not a newly converted man, for fear that he might get puffed up with pride and fall into the judgment passed upon the Devil. Moreover, he should also have a fine testimony from people on the outside, in order that he might not fall into reproach and a snare of the Devil."

Paul wrote to Titus: "For this reason I left you in Crete, that you might correct the things that were defective and might make appointments of older men in city after city, as I gave you orders; if there is any man free from accusation, a husband of one wife, having believing children that were not under a charge of debauchery nor unruly. For an overseer must be free from accusation as God's steward, not self-willed, not prone to wrath, not a drunken brawler, not a smiter, not greedy of dishonest gain, but hospitable, a lover of goodness, sound in mind, righteous, loyal, self-controlled, holding firmly to the faithful word as respects his art of teaching, that he may be able both to exhort by the teaching that is healthful and to reprove those who contradict." (Titus 1:5-9) Paul's counsel concerning overseers emphasizes what is involved in carrying out their responsibilities. Other Bible writers discuss additional Christian qualities required of men appointed as overseers, or shepherds, of the congregation. —Jas. 3:13, 17, 18.

Although the Scriptural requirements may at first seem to be somewhat overwhelming, there should be no reason for Christian men to shy away from desiring the fine work associated with the office of overseer. By taking the lead in manifesting fine Christian qualities, overseers encourage other members of the congregation to do the same. This is indicated by what the apostle Paul wrote in describing how "gifts in men" are provided "with a view to the readjustment of the holy ones, for ministerial work, for the building up of the body of the Christ, *until we all attain to the oneness in the faith and in the accurate knowledge of the Son of God, to a full-grown man, to the measure of stature that belongs to the fullness of the Christ."* (Eph. 4:8, 12, 13) Since all Christians are to strive to attain spiritual maturity, those standing before the congregation as appointed overseers are required to be taking the lead.

Paul instructed Timothy and Titus to appoint qualified men in the congregation to serve as overseers. They would *not* be mere boys or *newly converted* men, but they would be individuals with experience in Christian living, reflecting a broad knowledge of the Bible, a deep understanding of it, and a genuine love for the congregation. The overseers would be individuals who have the courage to speak up when wrongdoing exists and to take the needed action to correct it, thus protecting the flock from any who would selfishly exploit them. (Isa. 32:2) The overseers would be men readily recognized by all in the congregation as spiritually mature, having genuine concern for the flock of God. Their overall way of life would show this.

Those qualifying for appointment as overseers of the flock of God would be demonstrating a measure of practical wisdom in their daily lives. If married, they would be adhering to the Christian standard for marriage, namely, *husband of one wife,* and would be *presiding over their own household in a fine manner.* If the overseer has *believing children* who are *in subjection with all seriousness* and are *not under a charge of debauchery nor unruly,* other members of the congregation could confidently approach the overseer for counsel and advice on a wide range of personal matters having to do with family life and Christian living. Having conducted themselves properly within the family arrangement as well as within the community in general, these men would also be *irreprehensible,* be *free from accusation,* and *have a fine testimony* even *from people on the outside.* No valid charge of improper conduct could be brought against them to mar the reputation of the congregation. They would not have been reproved recently for serious wrongdoing. Others in the congregation would be moved to imitate this fine example and entrust their spiritual life to the shepherds' care.—1 Cor. 11:1; 16:15, 16; Phil. 2:25, 29; Heb. 13:7, 17.

Such qualified men would be able to serve the Christian congregation in a role similar to that of the older men of Israel who were described as "wise and discreet and experienced." (Deut. 1:13) They would not be without sin. (Rom. 3:23) But they would be known in the congregation and in the community as upright and God-fearing men who have demonstrated over a period of time that they conduct their entire life on the basis of God's principles. Their blamelessness would give them freeness of speech before the congregation.

Men qualifying for appointment as overseers would display *moderation in personal habits* and in their dealings with others. They would not be fanatics, but their way of life would be characterized by balance, *orderliness,* and *self-control.* Moderation would be demonstrated in such things as eating, drinking, recreation, hobbies, and entertainment. They would be moderate in the use of alcoholic beverages so as *not* to leave themselves open to charges of drunkenness or of being a *drunken brawler.* One whose senses have been dulled by intoxicating drink easily loses self-control and is not in a position to watch over the spiritual interests of the congregation.

Exercising oversight of the affairs of the congregation requires a man to demonstrate a measure of *or-*

derliness, being systematic in life, habits, and work. This includes his personal appearance, his home, and his personal activities. Such a man avoids procrastination, and he is able to see what is required and to plan accordingly. He adheres to theocratic order.

An overseer must be *reasonable.* He must be able to work in unity with and cooperate with others within the body of older men, who are charged with the oversight of the congregation. He should have a proper view of himself in relation to others, both inside and outside the congregation. As a reasonable person, the overseer would not be opinionated, always considering his views as superior to those of his fellow elders. Others may excel in qualities or abilities that he may lack. Reasonableness comes as a result of basing one's conclusions solidly on the Scriptures and of striving to imitate the example of Jesus Christ. (Phil. 2:2-8) By showing proper respect for others and considering others as superior to himself, an elder would *not become belligerent or be a smiter* of others, either physically or verbally. He would *not be self-willed,* always insisting that his way or his point of view must be accepted as best. He would *not be prone to wrath* but would be peaceable in his dealings with others.

Similarly, one qualifying to serve as an overseer in the congregation should be *sound in mind.* This means that he should have a good comprehension of Jehovah's principles and their application. He should be levelheaded, not hasty in judgment. He should be receptive to counsel and direction. He should not be double-minded, hypocritical, or fanatic.

Paul reminded Titus that an overseer should also be *a lover of goodness.* He should be *righteous* and *loyal.* These qualities would be reflected in his dealings with others and in his firm stand for what is right and good. He would be unwavering in his devotion to Jehovah and consistent in upholding righteous principles when making judgments. He would be able to keep a confidence.

As one who is sound in mind, of course, he would not be overly demanding in what he expects of others. Nor would the overseer be unduly concerned about material advantages for himself, *not greedy of dishonest gain, not a lover of money*. He would not use his office to take material advantage of the brothers under his care, nor would he hold back because of the reasonable material sacrifices he may be required to make in order to give generously of his time in caring for the needs of the congregation. His love for the brothers, as well as for strangers, and his self-sacrificing endeavors in their behalf would mean that he is genuinely *hospitable,* freely giving of himself and his belongings for the benefit of others. —Acts 20:33-35.

In order to carry out his assignment effectively, an overseer, or shepherd, of the congregation would need to be *qualified to teach*. According to Paul's words to Titus, the overseer would be *"holding firmly to the faithful word as respects his art of teaching, that he may be able both to exhort by the teaching that is healthful and to reprove those who contradict."* (Titus 1:9) In employing his art of teaching, the overseer would be able to reason with others, produce evidence, overcome objections, and apply the Scriptures in such a way that others would be convinced and have their faith strengthened. The overseer would be able to exercise such teaching ability under circumstances both favorable and unfavorable. (2 Tim. 4:2) He would have the patience needed to reprove with mildness one who is in error or to convince a doubter and move him to profitable works on the basis of faith. Being qualified to teach either before an audience or on a one-on-one basis would give evidence that the overseer meets this important requirement.

The apostle Peter wrote that the older men of the congregation should serve *willingly* and *eagerly,* neither under compulsion nor begrudgingly. They should be enthusiastic in their endeavors. They should be *taking the lead, becoming examples to the flock.*—Heb. 13:17.

All of this may seem like a great deal to expect of one who serves as an overseer. Certainly no overseer could measure up perfectly to the high standard set forth in the Bible, as outlined here, but none of the appointed elders in the congregation should be so significantly deficient in any one of these qualities that the deficiency could be considered a serious flaw. Some elders may have certain outstanding qualities, whereas others of the body may excel in a number of different qualities. The effect is that the body as a whole will have within itself all the fine qualities that are necessary for exercising proper oversight of the congregation of God.

When recommending men for appointment as overseers, the body of elders will want to keep in mind their own standing before Jehovah and their relationship with fellow Christians. Romans 12:3 counsels that each one should in no way "think more of himself than it is necessary to think; but to think so as to have a sound mind, each one as God has distributed to him a measure of faith." Each should consider himself a lesser one. None should prove to be "righteous overmuch" when examining the qualifications of another. (Eccl. 7:16) Having clearly in mind the Scriptural requirements for elders, the body would want to determine whether a brother being considered measures up to those standards to a reasonable degree or he is so seriously deficient in one or more of the Scriptural requirements that he does not qualify to serve. Allowing for human imperfections and being free of biased leanings and hypocrisy, appointed elders will make their recommendations in a manner showing due respect for Jehovah's righteous standards and for the good of the congregation. Like Timothy and Titus, elders today need to give prayerful consideration to each recommendation and follow the direction of God's holy spirit. This is one of the serious responsibilities they shoulder, and they must do so in accord with Paul's admonition 'never to lay their hands hastily upon any man.'—1 Tim. 5: 21, 22.

Men meeting the Christian standards for overseers are able to protect the congregation from spiritual dangers, and they serve as fine examples of Christian conduct for all to imitate. They have freeness of speech, enabling them to be bold in giving needed counsel to those within the congregation and to be zealous in proclaiming the good news in the field ministry.—Acts 4:29; 1 Tim. 3:13; Heb. 10:19-23, 35.

FRUITAGE OF THE SPIRIT

Spiritually qualified men would give evidence in their life that they are directed by holy spirit. They would be producing the fruitage of the spirit, described at Galatians 5:22, 23 as "love, joy, peace, long-suffering, kindness, goodness, faith, mildness, self-control." Their oversight of the congregation would be refreshing to the brothers and would serve to unite the congregation in rendering sacred service. Their course of conduct and the fruits of their labors would give evidence that they are appointed by holy spirit. (Acts 20:28) Having the spiritual requirements for overseers and shepherds stated so precisely in the inspired Scriptures has made it possible to have qualified men appointed to shepherd the flock today.

MEN WHO PROMOTE UNITY

It is vital that elders work together to promote unity in the congregation. While having personalities that vary widely, they preserve their unity by listening respectfully to one another even though they may not agree on every matter they discuss. As long as no Bible principle is being violated, each should be willing to yield and to support the final decision of the body of elders. A yielding spirit shows that one is guided by "the wisdom from above," which is "peaceable, reasonable." (Jas. 3:17, 18) No elder should think that he is above the others in the body, and no elder should try to dominate the others. Elders are really cooperating with Jehovah when they cooperate as a body for the good of the congregation. —1 Cor., chap. 12; Col. 2:19.

REACHING OUT

The office of overseer is to be desired by mature Christian men. (1 Tim. 3:1) However, the appointment means work and self-sacrifice. It means making oneself available to serve the needs of the brothers, caring for their spiritual interests. Reaching out for the office means striving to meet the qualifications set out in the Scriptures. The overseers of the congregation have both responsibility and accountability in caring for those entrusted to them.

Overseers take very seriously what is stated at Hebrews 13:17, where they are referred to as "those who are taking the lead," those who are "keeping watch over" the souls of the brothers, and "those who will render an account." Overseers must exercise special care not to 'lord it over' the flock of God, not to use their position of responsibility for selfish advantage, and not to serve because they feel that they are compelled to do so. The overseers must prove themselves to be loving shepherds of the flock of God.—1 Pet. 5:2, 3; Prov. 27:23.

Hebrews 13:17 gives direction also to members of the congregation when it says: "Be obedient to those who are taking the lead among you and be submissive, for they are keeping watch over your souls as those who will render an account; that they may do this with joy and not with sighing, for this would be damaging to you." Although the overseers are imperfect men, there is no need for anyone in the congregation to hold back from being submissive, since it is Jehovah's arrangement and He will hold the overseers accountable for their actions. They are representing him and his theocratic rule. Just as Jehovah uses holy spirit to appoint a man, by means of that same holy spirit, Jehovah will remove from office those overseers who fail to manifest the fruitage of the spirit and whose pattern of life falls short of the Scriptural requirements.

Do we not truly appreciate the hard work and fine example of the congregation overseers? In writing to the congregation at Thessalonica, Paul admonished the brothers: "We request you, brothers, to have regard for those who are working hard among you and presiding over you in the Lord and admonishing you; and to give them more than extraordinary consideration in love because of their work." (1 Thess. 5:12, 13) Much of the hard work of the congregation overseers makes our service to God easier and more enjoyable. Also, in his first letter to Timothy, Paul makes mention of the attitude that members of the congregation should cultivate toward the overseers, saying: "Let the older men who preside in a fine way be reckoned worthy of double honor, especially those who work hard in speaking and teaching."—1 Tim. 5:17.

PERSONAL CIRCUMSTANCES MAY CHANGE

Of course, a brother who has served faithfully for a period of time may become physically ill or otherwise incapacitated, perhaps because of advancing age, and may no longer be able to care for the responsibilities of an overseer as he once did or in the way that other overseers do. Even so, he should still be viewed and respected as an older man as long as he is appointed. There would be no need for him to step aside on account of his limitations. He is still worthy of the double honor given to all hardworking older men who are serving to the best of their respective abilities in shepherding the flock.

But if a brother should feel that it would be best for him to step aside because of changed personal circumstances that limit his ability to serve, he may choose to do so. (1 Pet. 5:2) He should still be viewed with respect and be able to do much good in the congregation, even though no longer having assignments and duties given to elders.

POSITIONS OF RESPONSIBILITY IN THE CONGREGATION

The Governing Body may arrange for men who qualify to serve as overseers in any locality at any time. The Governing Body is not bound by the recommendations of any local body of elders. Such recommendations serve merely as a guide and may even be rejected for reasons well-known to the Governing Body. Also, the Governing Body may authorize certain representatives to make appointments of overseers.—1 Tim. 1:3; Titus 1:5.

Whenever there are appointments or deletions of overseers, appropriate announcements are made to the congregation. This enables all concerned to know who are currently serving within the local congregation, and they can thus cooperate with the arrangement that is in effect.

Elders care for a variety of responsibilities in the congregation. There is a presiding overseer, a secretary, a service overseer, a *Watchtower* Study conductor, and a Theocratic Ministry School overseer. Some elders, if not all, serve as Congregation Book Study overseers. The elders serve in these positions for an indefinite period of time. Of course, if a brother holding any of these positions moves, is unable to care for his responsibilities because of health reasons, or becomes disqualified for failure to measure up to the Scriptural requirements, another elder is selected to handle the assignment. In congregations where the number of overseers is limited, it may be necessary for an elder to handle more than one assignment until other brothers qualify to be appointed as elders.

The presiding overseer serves as chairman at meetings of the body of elders. He should be a good organizer and able to preside in real earnest. (Rom. 12:8) He is responsible for overseeing the Service Meeting. He also arranges for public talks, at times using another elder or a well-qualified ministerial servant to assist him if needed.

The secretary handles congregation records and keeps the elders informed about important communications. If necessary, another elder or a capable ministerial servant may be assigned to assist in caring for some routine matters.

Arrangements for field activity and other service-related matters come under the direction of the service overseer. He schedules regular visits to all Congregation Book Study groups so that once each month he visits a different group and gives a service talk. On the weekend of his visit, he will work with the group in the field ministry and help publishers with their return visits and Bible studies. In smaller congregations where there are only one or two book studies, he may arrange to visit each one twice during the year.

The specific duties of these brothers, along with the *Watchtower* Study conductor, the Theocratic Ministry School overseer, Congregation Book Study overseers, and others who make up the body of elders, are set out from time to time in *Our Kingdom Ministry* and letters from the branch office.

Depending on the number available and their individual abilities, various elders handle assignments in connection with the other congregation meetings each week. These meetings are planned and prepared so that they will be informative and spiritually upbuilding. The elders are responsible for presenting instructive public talks. Besides teaching in the congregation, the elders take the lead in the field ministry, working along with the publishers.

It is suggested that the body of elders in each congregation meets periodically to discuss matters related to the spiritual progress of the congregation.

Two such meetings are held each year in conjunction with the regular visits of the circuit overseer. About three months after each visit of the circuit overseer, a meeting should be scheduled. These four meetings during the year are most likely sufficient for resolving any matters requiring the attention of the entire body of elders. Of course, the elders may convene at any time circumstances make it advisable. But if each one gives proper attention to his assigned duties and if the work of the elders is being adequately supervised and coordinated through the presiding overseer, meetings involving the entire body of elders can be kept to a minimum.

CONGREGATION SERVICE COMMITTEE

There are certain duties that are cared for by the Congregation Service Committee, made up of the presiding overseer, the secretary, and the service overseer. Members of this committee are involved in handling and signing various forms, such as those used in connection with literature inventories and requests, field service reports, and recommendations for appointment or removal of overseers, ministerial servants, and regular pioneers. In addition, the service committee approves the use of the Kingdom Hall for weddings and funerals and is responsible for assigning publishers to book study groups. It also approves applications for auxiliary pioneer service and other avenues of service. From time to time, the branch office calls upon the Congregation Service Committee to perform other duties. While elders on the service committee have been given certain authority to care for matters, these brothers work under the direction of the body of elders.

CONGREGATION BOOK STUDY OVERSEER

One of the outstanding privileges in the congregation is to serve as a Congregation Book Study overseer. Such overseers have the opportunity to help others in a number of areas. Because this responsibility is a serious one, elders should be used if available. If not, then one elder might care for more than one group, doing so at different times during the week. This, however, would depend on his circumstances. Or a capable ministerial servant can be used until such time as an elder can take over. A ministerial servant working in this capacity is called a Congregation Book Study servant, as he does not function as an overseer in the congregation. Rather, he works under the direction of the elders in caring for his responsibility. How a ministerial servant is used is something for the elders to decide. They also decide to which group the elder or ministerial servant is assigned.

One of the chief responsibilities of the Congregation Book Study overseer is to conduct the Congregation Book Study. In order to do so adequately, he must prepare thoroughly. He should know not only the answers to the study questions but also the reasons behind those answers and the value of the material. It should be his goal to help the group get a clear understanding of what is being considered so that they can apply the truths learned to their own life as well as explain them to others. This requires a conscientious effort on his part, even as emphasized by Paul as found at Romans 12:7: "He that teaches, let him be at his teaching."

Another important feature of the book study overseer's work is that of taking the lead in the field ministry. The regularity, zeal, and enthusiasm that he shows in the field activity will be reflected in the publishers. Because the brothers appreciate the encouragement and help that come through being together, a group witnessing schedule convenient for the majority should be worked out and maintained. (Luke 10:1-16) The overseer needs to plan so that there is always enough territory to work. He will conduct the meeting for field service and organize the publishers for that day's work. When he cannot be there, he should arrange for another elder, a ministerial servant or, if neither is available, a qualified publisher to care for these responsibilities so that the publishers have the good leadership they need.

The service overseer is a real help to the book study overseer and the entire group. A wise book study overseer will plan ahead for the visit of the service overseer, informing his group of the visit and building anticipation for its benefits. When all in the group are kept fully aware of the arrangement, they can enthusiastically support it. There will be a corresponding improvement in their field activity.

Each book study group is purposely kept small. This allows the book study overseer to become well acquainted with all assigned to it. As a loving shepherd, he is keenly interested in each one. He tries to give personal help and encouragement for the field ministry, for support of congregation meetings, and for whatever else is appropriate to help each person keep spiritually strong. Those who become ill or depressed will benefit from a personal visit. An encouraging suggestion or a word of counsel might prompt some to reach out for additional privileges in the congregation and thus become of greater use to their brothers. While most of the book study overseer's efforts will logically be directed toward helping those in his own group, as an elder and a shepherd, he will have the entire congregation in mind. He is lovingly concerned for all and is ready to help any who are in need.—Acts 20:17, 28.

A responsibility of the Congregation Book Study overseer is to assist in collecting field service reports from the publishers and pioneers in his book study group. These reports are then given, along with the book study attendance figures, to the secretary for compiling. Individual publishers can assist the book study overseer by turning in their field service reports promptly. This can be done by submitting their reports directly to the book study overseer at the end of each month or by placing them in the box designated for service reports at the Kingdom Hall.

POSITIONS OF RESPONSIBILITY IN THE ORGANIZATION

At times, selected elders are appointed to serve on Hospital Liaison Committees and as members of Patient Visitation Groups. These men visit hospitals and doctors to encourage continued and expanded treatment of Jehovah's Witnesses without using blood. Other overseers are able to advance Kingdom interests by serving as members of Regional Building Committees, Assembly Hall Committees, or district convention committees. The hard work of these brothers and their willingness to expend themselves in this way are very much appreciated by all in the organization. Indeed, we 'hold men of that sort dear.' —Phil. 2:29.

CITY OVERSEER

The branch office will appoint a city overseer in cities where there is more than one congregation.

Usually, this appointment is made on the recommendation of the circuit overseer or circuit overseers if more than one serves congregations in that city. The city overseer does not exercise jurisdiction in any congregation other than the one in which he serves as an elder. The branch office may wish to communicate with him on various matters, such as arrangements for assemblies and schools that may be held in his city. However, the branch deals directly with each congregation in regard to literature supplies, monthly field service reports, and other matters.

CIRCUIT OVERSEER

The Governing Body arranges for the appointment of qualified elders to serve as circuit overseers. These are assigned by the branch office to visit the congregations that make up their circuits on a regular basis, usually twice a year. They also periodically visit pioneers, special pioneers, or missionaries serving in isolated territory. They plan their routing and notify each congregation sufficiently in advance so that the visit will result in the most benefit.

The presiding overseer takes the lead in organizing matters so that the visit will prove spiritually refreshing to all. (Rom. 1:11, 12) After he receives notification of the visit and information about the needs of the circuit overseer and (if married) his wife, the presiding overseer makes arrangements through various brothers to get literature supplies, accommodations, and other necessary things. He makes sure that all, including the circuit overseer, are informed of these arrangements.

The circuit overseer will contact the presiding overseer regarding the scheduling of meetings, including meetings for field service. These will be arranged in accord with local circumstances and the circuit overseer's suggestions as well as what is directed in *Our Kingdom Ministry* and in letters from the branch office. All need to be informed in advance concerning the times of the meetings with the congregation, with the pioneers, and with the elders and ministerial servants, as well as the places and times of meetings for field service. This will enable all to adjust their affairs so that they can benefit from the entire week's activities.

Since the circuit overseer will check the congregation records on Tuesday afternoon, such records should be in good order and available before he arrives. The presiding overseer will be sure to have them at the location where they will be checked. It is helpful if a member of the Congregation Service Committee can be present to render any assistance needed. The circuit overseer will examine the *Congregation's Publisher Record* cards, meeting attendance records, territory records, and the accounts. This will give him some insight into possible needs of the congregation and how he may be of assistance to those responsible for keeping these records.

During his visit, the circuit overseer takes time to speak with the brothers individually as he is able—at meetings, out in the field service, at mealtimes, and otherwise. Additionally, he meets with the elders and ministerial servants, sharing appropriate Scriptural counsel, suggestions, and encouragement that will help them shoulder their responsibilities in serving and shepherding the flock in their care. (Prov. 27:23; Acts 20:26-32; 1 Tim. 4:11-16) He also meets with the pioneers to encourage them in their work and to give personal assistance regarding any problems they may be encountering in their ministry.

If there are other matters that need attention, the circuit overseer will either handle these or assist the elders to the extent possible while he is visiting the congregation. He will strive to help the elders or individuals involved to locate the Scriptural direction that applies. If there has been some serious wrongdoing and the elders need his assistance in handling such, he will set aside time for this purpose. If there is anything that the branch office needs to do in following through, he and the elders will provide the branch with a detailed report on the matter.

While visiting the congregation, the circuit overseer attends the regular congregation meetings. These may be adjusted from time to time in harmony with directions in *Our Kingdom Ministry* or letters from the branch office. He will give several talks designed to encourage, motivate, instruct, and fortify the congregation. He will strive to foster love and appreciation for Jehovah, Jesus Christ, and the organization. The circuit overseer will also encourage zealous participation in field service, providing practical suggestions on how to do the work effectively.

One of the primary objectives of the circuit overseer's visit is to provide leadership in field service. Many in the congregation may be able to adjust their schedule so that they can have a fuller share in field service that week. Some may be able to arrange to auxiliary pioneer the month of his visit. Those desirous of working with him or his wife can make an appointment through the presiding overseer. Much good can be accomplished by taking the circuit overseer or his wife on Bible studies and return visits. At times, adjustments in your schedule may have to be made, but the benefits are worth it. The circuit overseer is encouraged to arrange for an early start in field service each day, taking local circumstances into consideration. Your extra effort to give full support to this aspect of the week's visit is deeply appreciated.—Prov. 27:17.

Every year a circuit assembly and a special assembly day are arranged for each circuit. The circuit overseer is responsible for the operation of the assembly organization on these occasions. On the circuit overseer's recommendation, the branch office appoints permanent assembly personnel: an assembly overseer and an assistant assembly overseer. They are to work closely with the circuit overseer in caring for the assembly organization. This will enable the circuit overseer to give his primary attention to the assembly program. The circuit overseer designates other capable men to care for various departments. He also arranges for an audit of the circuit accounts after each assembly.

The circuit overseer reports his field service directly to the branch office at the end of each month. He is also reimbursed for certain modest expenses incurred, such as travel, food, lodging, and other necessary items required to carry out his work if the congregations do not cover these. Traveling representatives have confidence that as Jesus promised, material needs will be provided if they seek continually the interests of Jehovah's Kingdom. (Luke 12:31) The congregations will want to be conscious of their privilege to display hospitality to these devoted elders who serve them.—3 John 5-8.

DISTRICT OVERSEER

The district overseer is also an appointed traveling elder. He is assigned by the branch office to serve a number of circuits that make up a district. He serves as chairman of the circuit assembly programs in his district and gives the public discourse on such programs. The first part of each week in which a circuit assembly is held, he works with the host congregation in the circuit being served. He takes the lead in group witnessing and gives an upbuilding Scriptural talk to the host congregation.

The branch office assigns each circuit the dates for its circuit assembly and special assembly day and notifies the district overseer of this schedule, which he then follows as his assigned routing. Because of distances involved for the publishers or the small size of assembly facilities, some circuits are divided into sections with a circuit assembly or a special assembly day held for each section. The district overseer is informed of this and plans to spend a week in the circuit for each circuit assembly to be held. In advance, he works out with the circuit overseer which congregation can appropriately be the host congregation for each circuit assembly.

On Tuesday afternoon of his visit, the district overseer gives encouragement to the circuit overseer and (if married) his wife and offers helpful suggestions to assist them with their work. From time to time, the branch office will outline points to be discussed at this meeting. The circuit overseer and his wife may have matters with which they desire assistance. (Prov. 20:5) The district overseer may have points to share based on things he has learned through experience and observation. Privately, the circuit overseer will discuss the needs of the circuit with the district overseer, who may decide to work some of these points into his talks on the circuit assembly program.

During the first part of the week with the host congregation, usually on Tuesday evening, the district overseer will attend an abbreviated Congregation Book Study and give a talk to the congregation. If the elders need advice or assistance with some congregation matters, they will let him know this in advance, and he will meet with them. Primarily, he will take the lead in group witnessing during the week. He and his wife will have a full schedule of field service. The circuit overseer and his wife will also give full support to the field service activity that week. The presiding overseer will make sure that all are informed of the arrangements for meetings for service. He will also see that adequate territory is available and make appointments on behalf of any who have requested to work with the traveling overseers.

At the conclusion of the circuit assembly (or assemblies), the district overseer will send the branch office a report on how the program was presented and received in that circuit. He will report on the spiritual condition and the needs of the circuit. Once a month, he also reports his field service and expenses. His accommodations and expenses are cared for in the same way as for the circuit overseer.

BRANCH COMMITTEE

In each branch office of Jehovah's Witnesses throughout the world, three or more spiritually qualified and mature brothers serve as a Branch Committee to oversee the preaching work in the country or countries under their jurisdiction. One of the committee members serves as the Branch Committee coordinator.

Those serving on the Branch Committee handle matters pertaining to all the congregations in their territory. They arrange for the distribution of publications furnished by "the faithful and discreet slave" to strengthen all associated with the congregations. (Matt. 24:45) Their primary objective is to see to it that the good news of the Kingdom is preached throughout the territory assigned and that congregations, circuits, and districts are set up to give proper oversight to the needs of the field. The Branch Committee also gives attention to the missionary field and to special, regular, and auxiliary pioneer activity. When there are assemblies and conventions, these brothers make arrangements and assignments to ensure that "all things take place decently and by arrangement."—1 Cor. 14:40.

A Country Committee is appointed in some lands that come under the oversight of a Branch Committee in another land. This allows for closer supervision of the work where the Country Committee serves. It cares for matters in the Bethel Home and office, handles correspondence and reports, and generally cares for the activities in the field. The Country Committee cooperates with the Branch Committee for the advancement of the Kingdom.

The Governing Body makes all appointments of those selected to serve as members of Branch Committees and Country Committees.

ZONE OVERSEER

Periodically, arrangements are made by the Governing Body to have qualified brothers visit each of the branches throughout the earth. Brothers serving in this capacity are known as zone overseers.

Their primary work is to help the Branch Committee with problems or questions they may have in carrying on the preaching and disciple-making work. Wherever practical, the zone overseer also meets with the missionaries who work under the branches he visits. He talks with them about their problems and needs, giving necessary encouragement regarding their most important activity, Kingdom preaching and disciple making.

The zone overseer also examines the various records that are kept for operating a branch office. He is especially interested in what is being accomplished in the field as far as the Kingdom preaching and other congregation activities are concerned. If there is a printery, farm, or other facility, he inspects each of these operations. When the zone overseer visits branches, he also shares to the extent possible in the Kingdom-preaching work.

LOVING OVERSIGHT

Visits by traveling overseers provide an interchange of encouragement, and the congregations are thus made firm in the faith. (Rom. 1:12; Eph. 4:3) The publishers are made aware of their interdependency. They work for the common good of all and cooperate in spreading the Kingdom good news. (1 Cor. 12:12-31) Certainly we have benefited greatly from the hard work and loving care of mature Christian men. We will benefit even further as we continue submitting ourselves to congregation elders and other appointed overseers charged with shepherding the flock and overseeing the work. (1 Cor. 16:15-18; Phil. 2:25, 29) As we do this, we are drawn into unity with the Head of the congregation, Christ Jesus, our Lord, the one appointed by Jehovah as the Fine Shepherd. (Eph. 1:22, 23) As a result, God's spirit permeates the congregations worldwide, and God's Word serves to guide the work throughout the earth. —Ps. 119:105.

CHAPTER 6

MINISTERIAL SERVANTS RENDER VALUABLE SERVICE

TO THE congregation at Philippi, the apostle Paul wrote: "Paul and Timothy, slaves of Christ Jesus, to all the holy ones in union with Christ Jesus who are in Philippi, along with overseers and ministerial servants." (Phil. 1:1) Note that in his salutation, he made mention of the ministerial servants. These men evidently fulfilled an important role in assisting the elders in the congregation back then. The same is true in our time. Ministerial servants render a number of services that help the overseers and that contribute to the good order of the congregation.

Have you become acquainted with the ministerial servants in your congregation? Are you aware of the many fine services they perform for your benefit and for the benefit of the entire congregation? The apostle specifically mentions them and states: "The men who minister in a fine manner are acquiring for themselves a fine standing and great freeness of speech in the faith in connection with Christ Jesus." —1 Tim. 3:13.

SCRIPTURAL REQUIREMENTS FOR MINISTERIAL SERVANTS

Ministerial servants are expected to lead a wholesome Christian life, be responsible men, and give proof that they are able to care for assignments properly. This becomes obvious when we consider what Paul had to say in his letter to Timothy about the qualifications of ministerial servants: “Ministerial servants should likewise be serious, not double-tongued, not giving themselves to a lot of wine, not greedy of dishonest gain, holding the sacred secret of the faith with a clean conscience. Also, let these be tested as to fitness first, then let them serve as ministers, as they are free from accusation. Let ministerial servants be husbands of one wife, presiding in a fine manner over children and their own households. For the men who minister in a fine manner are acquiring for themselves a fine standing and great freeness of speech in the faith in connection with Christ Jesus.”—1 Tim. 3:8-10, 12, 13.

The work of ministerial servants generally involves nonteaching responsibilities. By their hard work and exemplary Christian life, they not only perform vital services for the congregation but also set an example to be imitated by others.—1 Tim. 4:11, 12.

The specific Scriptural requirements for ministerial servants mentioned by Paul in his first letter to Timothy indicate that a high standard is set for men who are used in this capacity. Holding to such a standard serves to protect the congregation from any legitimate accusation as to the kind of men to whom it entrusts special responsibilities. Whether younger or older in years, ministerial servants are expected to be active in the ministry each month, setting a fine example. They should be exemplary in their dress, grooming, speech, attitude, and conduct. Such a pattern of living with soundness of mind gains the respect of others and reflects the seriousness with which ministerial servants view their relationship with Jehovah and their privileges of service in the congregation.—Titus 2:2, 6-8.

These are men who have been "tested as to fitness." Even before receiving their appointment, they proved to be truly dedicated men, whose faith has been made manifest in carrying on zealous Kingdom service and in helping others to be made firm in the faith. In their response to the good news, they have demonstrated that they put Kingdom interests first in their life and are reaching out for whatever service privileges may be open to them. They are indeed examples for others in the congregation to imitate. —1 Tim. 3:10.

HOW THEY SERVE

Ministerial servants render a variety of practical services in behalf of their brothers and sisters. In doing so, they are helpful to the overseers, relieving them of detailed work, thus leaving them free to care for teaching and shepherding responsibilities. In making the service assignments, the elders take into account the number of appointed ministerial servants in the congregation as well as their individual abilities.

Just consider some of the services they perform. One ministerial servant may be assigned to take care of the congregation literature, making it convenient for us to obtain the literature we need for our personal use and for the field ministry. Another may care for the magazines. Others are assigned to keep records, such as for congregation accounts or for territory, or they are assigned to handle microphones, to operate sound equipment, to look after the platform, or perhaps to help the elders in other ways. There is much work to be done in maintaining the Kingdom

Hall and keeping it clean, so ministerial servants are often called upon to assist in caring for these responsibilities. Ministerial servants are also assigned to serve as attendants, to welcome new ones, and to help maintain order at congregation meetings.

In some congregations, there may be enough ministerial servants for a different one to be assigned to each of these duties. Elsewhere, a ministerial servant may care for several assignments. In some instances, it is beneficial to have more than one person assigned to do certain work. If there are not enough ministerial servants to care for some of these responsibilities, the body of elders may arrange for other exemplary baptized brothers to care for some of this necessary work. Thus they would gain experience that would be useful later when they, in turn, become qualified to be appointed as ministerial servants. Or if brothers are not available, certain sisters who show godly humility and devotion to Jehovah could be asked to assist with some things even though, of course, they would not be appointed as ministerial servants.

Periodically, if there is good reason, elders may find it beneficial to change some assignments from one ministerial servant to another. However, there is great advantage in having brothers continue to handle the same assignments in order to become more proficient and to gain experience. How the elders work out these assignments handled by ministerial servants would be according to the congregation's needs.

Depending on local circumstances, there may be other services that can be assigned to ministerial servants who are doing as the apostle Paul encouraged young Timothy, 'making their spiritual advancement manifest.' (1 Tim. 4:15) If there are not enough elders to conduct the Congregation Book Studies, some of the more qualified ministerial servants may be used as Congregation Book Study servants to care for assigned groups. They may be assigned to handle parts in the Service Meeting and on the Theocratic Ministry School and to deliver public talks in the local congregation. Other privileges may be extended to some of the ministerial servants when there is a particular need and if they meet the requirements for the assignment.—1 Pet. 4:10.

In assisting the elders, ministerial servants should give of themselves willingly, demonstrating that they have a sense of responsibility and are working for the advancement of Kingdom interests and for the benefit of everyone in the congregation. By taking the lead in the field service, ministerial servants can set a good example for others and reap great satisfaction themselves in a work well-done.

Though their work differs from that of the elders, it is no less a part of sacred service to God and is important to the smooth functioning of the congregation. In time, if ministerial servants discharge their obligations well and also become qualified to serve as shepherds and teachers, they may be recommended to serve as elders.

If you have not done so already, why not make a special effort to get acquainted with the ministerial servants in your congregation? You can show your appreciation for their hard work by cooperating with them as they care for their assigned duties. In this way, you will also be showing appreciation for Jehovah's provision for maintaining an orderly household. (Gal. 6:10) The ministerial servants are appointed by holy spirit for your good.

CHAPTER 7

MEETINGS THAT "INCITE TO LOVE AND FINE WORKS"

HOW fitting that arrangements are made for Christians to meet regularly for worship and to be fed spiritually! It is important for all of us to gather together to hear God's Word so as to learn his requirements and how we may serve him. This applies to both younger and older ones, just as it did in the case of God's ancient covenant people, the nation of Israel. Regarding every seventh Festival of Booths, Jehovah commanded the nation through Moses: "Congregate the people, the men and the women and the little ones and your alien resident who is within your gates, in order that they may listen and in order that they may learn, as they must fear Jehovah your God and take care to carry out all the words of this law."—Deut. 31:12.

Clearly, the purpose for meeting together now, even as it was then, is to listen and to learn and to be "taught by Jehovah." (Isa. 54:13) Assembling for worship in ancient Israel was always a joyous occasion, as reflected in the words of David, who wrote: "I rejoiced when they were saying to me: 'To the house of Jehovah let us go.'" (Ps. 122:1) The apostle Paul referred to an additional cause for joy when meeting with fellow worshipers. He wrote: "Let us consider one another to incite to love and fine works." (Heb. 10:24) Congregation meetings provided early Christians with the opportunity to get to know one another, to impart encouragement, and to gain strength through association. This is also true of Jehovah's Witnesses today as they meet together to worship Jehovah.

CONGREGATION MEETINGS

The Bible emphasizes the value of coming together to worship and praise Jehovah. (Ps. 26:8, 12; Matt. 18:20) Those who embraced the truth at Pentecost 33 C.E. did not treat this matter lightly. They continued devoting themselves to the teaching of the apostles, and "day after day they were in constant attendance at the temple with one accord." (Acts 2:42, 46) Later when Christians came together for worship, they read from inspired writings, including letters written by the apostles and other Christian disciples. (1 Cor. 1:1, 2; Col. 4:16; 1 Thess. 1:1; Jas. 1:1) There was congregation prayer. (Acts 4:24-29; 20:36) At times, experiences from the missionary field were related. (Acts 11:5-18; 14:27, 28) Bible doctrines and the fulfillment of inspired prophecies were considered. Instruction was given in matters of approved Christian conduct and godly devotion. All were encouraged to be zealous proclaimers of the good news.—Rom. 10:9, 10; 1 Cor. 11:23-26; 15:58; Eph. 5:1-33.

In our day Christian meetings in many respects follow the pattern set in apostolic days. We heed the inspired exhortation found at Hebrews 10:25 by "not forsaking the gathering of ourselves together, as some have the custom, but encouraging one another, and all the more so as [we] behold the day drawing near." During the difficult last days of this wicked system of things, we need the added encouragement that comes from regularly meeting together in order to maintain spiritual strength and Christian integrity. (Rom. 1:11, 12) As in Paul's day, Christians today live among a crooked and twisted generation. We have repudiated the ungodliness and worldly spirit of this system of things. (Phil. 2:

15, 16; Titus 2:12-14) Really, where would we rather be than in association with Jehovah's people? (Ps. 84:10) And what could be more beneficial than hearing the Word of God discussed?

Jehovah is the Source of an abundance of satisfying spiritual food. (Ps. 145:14, 15) Through his Son and "the faithful and discreet slave," food at the proper time is being dispensed. (Matt. 24:45) How is such provision served to the individual members of the organization? One means is through the various meetings held each week in the congregation. Consider these meetings and the benefits derived as we regularly 'incite one another to love and fine works.'

THE *WATCHTOWER* STUDY

The Watchtower Announcing Jehovah's Kingdom is the principal means to keep Jehovah's people well supplied with timely spiritual food. Certain articles published in *The Watchtower* are specifically prepared for weekly congregation study, with special instruction based on the written Word of God. Information carefully examined in the *Watchtower* Study stirs the hearts and minds of members of the congregation and builds up their spiritual strength.

The study articles are varied as to subject matter. The material frequently deals with the application of Bible principles in daily living and fortifies Christians against "the spirit of the world" and unclean conduct. (1 Cor. 2:12) Through the columns of *The Watchtower* come increased light on Bible doctrine and the discussion of fulfillment of prophecy as Jehovah makes this known, thus enabling all to keep abreast of the truth and stay on the path of the righteous ones. (Ps. 97:11; Prov. 4:18) Attending the *Watchtower* Study and participating in it can help us to rejoice in the hope of Jehovah's righteous new system of things. (Rom. 12:12; 2 Pet. 3:13) It helps us to manifest the fruitage of the spirit in our life and to keep strong our desire to serve Jehovah zealously. (Gal. 5:22, 23) It helps to strengthen our faith to endure trials and to build "a fine foundation for the future" so that we "may get a firm hold on the real life."—1 Tim. 6:19; 1 Pet. 1:6, 7.

It is evident that the material considered week by week at the *Watchtower* Study is vital. It helps us to grow spiritually, to make the truth of God's Word our own, to bring our life into harmony with the teachings of the Bible, and to be united spiritually with our brothers worldwide. What can each one do to take full advantage of this provision for spiritual feeding? Prepare the lesson in advance, looking up all cited scriptures, and have a share in commenting during the meeting. Such participation will cause the points under discussion to make a deeper impression, sounding down the truth into our heart. At the same time, others benefit as they hear our expressions of faith and hope. Carefully listening to their comments will ensure that we get the most benefit from the lesson each week.

The *Watchtower* Study helps us to maintain spiritual strength and firmness in the faith. It should not be looked upon as just routine. None should miss this important provision that Jehovah has made for strengthening all associated with the household of faith.

PUBLIC MEETING

The Public Meeting is usually held in conjunction with the weekly *Watchtower* Study, but it differs as to the method used in presenting information.

Whereas the *Watchtower* Study is developed as a question-and-answer discussion with audience participation, the Public Meeting features a discourse on a Bible subject. Such meetings play an important part in filling the spiritual needs of both new ones and members of the congregation.—Acts 18:4; 19: 9, 10.

By inviting interested ones as well as the public in general, we may accomplish much in acquainting people with basic Bible information. The Public Meeting helps one and all to remain alert to Christian teachings and encourages steadfastness in Kingdom service.

The subjects considered at the Public Meeting are varied. Talks cover Bible doctrine and prophecy as well as Scriptural principles and counsel regarding family life, marital matters, situations confronting youths, and Christian morals. Some talks center on Jehovah's marvelous works of creation. Others highlight the exemplary faith, courage, and integrity of different Bible characters, focusing on lessons for our day. The Public Meeting is truly an occasion for taking in informative and refreshing spiritual food.

If we are to get the full benefit of the Public Meeting arrangement, it is essential that we attend regularly, pay close attention, look up the scriptures referred to by the speaker, and follow along as he reads and explains them. (Luke 8:18) This will help us to become more familiar with the location of Bible books and will increase our knowledge of the Scriptures. As we thus make sure of the things discussed, we should be determined to hold fast to what we learn and to apply it personally.—1 Thess. 5:21.

If there are a sufficient number of speakers available, the congregation will no doubt have a public talk every week. Frequently, this is made possible by having speakers visit from nearby congregations. If there is a shortage of speakers in an area, arrangements are made to have these talks as often as possible.

Christ Jesus, his apostles, and their associates conducted public meetings similar to those enjoyed today by congregations of Jehovah's Witnesses. Without question, Jesus was the greatest public speaker ever on earth. It was said concerning him: "Never has another man spoken like this." (John 7:46) Jesus spoke with authority, astounding his audiences. (Matt. 7:28, 29) Many were the benefits received by those who took his message to heart. (Matt. 13:16, 17) The apostles followed his example. At Acts 2:22-36, we read of Peter's powerful discourse on the day of Pentecost 33 C.E. Many were motivated to act as a result of what they heard. Later, individuals benefited from Paul's discourse in Athens. (Acts 17:22-34) Similarly, in our day millions have received benefits through the weekly Public Meetings held in congregations as well as public talks presented at circuit assemblies and at district, national, and international conventions. We should give full support to the arrangement for Public Meetings.

SERVICE MEETING

The Service Meeting focuses on our field ministry. It equips us to have a full share in preaching the Kingdom good news, making disciples, and declaring the approaching execution of divine judgment. (Matt. 28:20; Mark 13:10; 2 Pet. 3:7) To a large extent, this work is done by speaking to people individually and providing them with Bible literature. But the application of Jehovah’s righteous principles in our life has a direct bearing on the effectiveness of our field ministry and the fruitage that we produce. (Matt. 13:23; John 15:8) We thereby demonstrate the good results that come from applying the Scriptures. Appropriately, the Service Meeting gives attention to all these facets of our service to God.

Each month *Our Kingdom Ministry* outlines the weekly Service Meetings. You will receive a copy through the congregation. When a new issue of *Our Kingdom Ministry* is received, the presiding overseer carefully analyzes what it contains and assigns the various meeting parts to qualified brothers. He may arrange for such assignments to be made through one of the other elders.

Elders and well-qualified ministerial servants are assigned to handle the various parts on the Service Meeting program. They should be careful, not to introduce additional material, but to develop the program parts as outlined in *Our Kingdom Ministry*. This means that they need to study the assigned material carefully to determine what the principal points of instruction are and how to handle them so that the brothers will understand and remember them. Careful thought is also given to application of the material to the situation of the local congregation.

While there are various ways that material can effectively be presented, in no case should the method of presentation overshadow the material presented. Demonstrations should not be dramatic productions with a lot of stage props. Use natural settings, such as a scene at one's secular work, a door-to-door call, a home Bible study, or a family discussion. Settings should fit what is encountered locally so that the publishers can relate to them.

Exemplary baptized publishers and their well-trained minor children may be asked to participate in certain parts, such as demonstrations. They may be interviewed or invited to relate their experiences. If you have an opportunity to participate, cooperate joyfully and conscientiously, recognizing that this is part of your service to Jehovah.

It should be the heartfelt desire of each Christian to live in a way that encourages others to follow Jesus Christ as dedicated Witnesses of Jehovah. To that end, Service Meeting programs are designed to reach the following objectives: (1) to encourage us to participate in the public ministry to the fullest extent possible—whether witnessing from house to house, on the street, or wherever people may be found—and to improve in our presentation of the good news; (2) to teach us how to make return visits on individuals who show interest or accept Bible literature; (3) to motivate us to set aside time for regularly conducting home Bible studies and directing students to the organization; (4) to give us ideas on how to witness informally; (5) to show us how to improve in our efforts to help new ones, our children, and other young people to become dedicated disciples.

You will benefit if before the meeting, you go over the program outlined in *Our Kingdom Ministry*. At times, articles in various publications of Jehovah's Witnesses are considered. Not only will advance research be informative but such research will also equip you to have a share when parts on the program call for audience participation. The more you absorb from the Service Meeting, the more effective you will be in your ministry.

When all in the congregation attend the Service Meeting regularly, unified activity is the result. Since every baptized Witness is a minister, attending this meeting is essential to help us carry out our commission. It is also very beneficial for anyone who desires to become a dedicated servant of God. Make attendance at this meeting part of your weekly schedule of activity.

Meetings of this sort are nothing new. They are based on sound Scriptural precedent. Before sending his disciples out to preach, Jesus gave them detailed instructions on what to say and do. (Matt. 10:5–11:1; Luke 10:1-16) Later his disciples continued to have such meetings at which they discussed their experiences in the ministry, and this strengthened them for zealous Kingdom activity. (Acts 4:23-31) We continue that same practice today.

THEOCRATIC MINISTRY SCHOOL

The Theocratic Ministry School is an ongoing provision for the education of all in the congregation. The curriculum includes Bible readings, Bible talks, student presentations, and other training for the field ministry. Counsel is given to students to help them progressively improve in their presentations. While offering a variety of information that is of interest and benefit to the entire congregation, the Theocratic Ministry School also gives participants as well as those in the audience opportunity to improve various aspects of their personal ministry. Occasional reviews provide a means of self-examination regarding individual progress in ministerial training.

Each year Jehovah's organization provides a Theocratic Ministry School Schedule setting out the program to be followed. This schedule outlines the material to be used and how the assignments are to be handled. For many years the Theocratic Ministry School has proved its worth in training Jehovah's Witnesses to be effective proclaimers of the Kingdom. All who are actively associated with the congregation, including people newly attending the meetings, may enroll as long as they agree with the teachings of the Bible and their life is in harmony with Christian principles.

By enrolling in the Theocratic Ministry School, we show that we are interested in spiritual advancement. The instruction there can help us to demonstrate "fine works" as public praisers of Jehovah. (Matt. 5:16) It can equip us to accomplish more in the time we have available for the field service and to incite others to action by our fine comments at the congregation meetings. In the case of brothers, this instruction will greatly assist them in qualifying as ministerial servants or elders and eventually in handling major Service Meeting parts and in giving public talks.

Those enrolled will be notified well in advance concerning their student assignments so that they can prepare thoroughly. When we have a part in the school, it is particularly important to be on hand before the meeting starts. We should make every effort to be present to fulfill our assignment. However, if on occasion an emergency arises and it is impossible for us to care for our part, we should immediately notify the school overseer or the brother assigned to assist him so that arrangements can be made for a substitute.

As a regular part of our spiritual feeding program, the Theocratic Ministry School provides many benefits. The prophet Isaiah said: "The Sovereign Lord Jehovah himself has given me the tongue of the taught ones, that I may know how to answer the tired one with a word." (Isa. 50:4) Unquestionably, the school has played an important part in training millions to develop the tongue of one taught by Jehovah. Over the years, this program has helped those enrolled to make spiritual advancement and to learn how better to express themselves in presenting the good news of the Kingdom. Under the direction of holy spirit, such training has enabled God's people to give an answer to everyone demanding a reason for their hope. Being taught to use God's Word in this way is a blessing.

Those enrolled in the Theocratic Ministry School can benefit greatly from the use of the Kingdom Hall library. The library should contain the available publications of Jehovah's Witnesses, *Watch Tower Publications Indexes,* perhaps a number of Bible translations, a concordance, and other helpful reference works. We should feel free to use any of these publications at the Kingdom Hall before or after the meetings.

CONGREGATION BOOK STUDY

Members of the congregation and others who are associated derive great personal benefit from the Congregation Book Study, a meeting generally conducted with a smaller group than at the other meetings. A few families and a small number of other individuals gather at each of these studies. Study groups meet in convenient locations scattered throughout the congregation territory, usually private homes. The Kingdom Hall may also be used for this purpose.

In some respects, these group studies provide benefits that do not directly come through other provisions of the congregation. Why is this so? It is because the Congregation Book Study arrangement provides not only for making a careful and detailed study of Bible subjects but also for giving more personal attention to the spiritual growth of each individual in these small groups. Such personal assistance may include appropriate Scriptural counsel, encouragement and direction for carrying out the ministry, as well as other vital spiritual help to fit the needs of the individual. This assistance is a reflection of Jehovah's loving-kindness and his tender care for his people.—Isa. 40:11.

The Congregation Book Study overseer is a student of God's Word and is qualified to help others to increase in Bible knowledge and to apply this knowledge in practical ways. Besides conducting the lesson, he shows personal interest in the physical and spiritual well-being of all in the group, assists them in the preaching work, and makes shepherding calls on them and on others in the congregation as the need arises. A capable ministerial servant may conduct the book study if an elder is not available.

This meeting is a group study using the Bible and a textbook provided by Jehovah's Witnesses. Basically, it is conducted in the same manner as the *Watchtower* Study. The book study is opened and closed with prayer, paragraphs are read, questions are asked on the paragraphs, comments are given, and scriptures are read as time permits. To impress principal thoughts on the mind of each one, the conductor may include a brief oral review at the end of the study. As we attend week by week, we will gain both knowledge and understanding. We will learn the reasons for statements that are made in the publication and how to support them from the Bible as well as how to conduct discussions of the same material with others whom we are able to help in our field ministry. (2 Tim. 2:15) This meeting will do much to equip us to become better teachers of God's Word.

In a small group such as this, there are more opportunities for us to offer comments. Thus, all of us, including new ones, have the opportunity to get accustomed to making a public declaration of our faith before others. (Heb. 13:15) It is good to learn to comment in our own words instead of reading out of the book.

Whereas anyone present may share in the reading of the scriptures, just one person is assigned to read the paragraphs. The Congregation Book Study overseer will arrange in advance for a baptized brother who is a good reader to read the paragraphs. Each week, a different qualified brother may be assigned to read the paragraphs. If no capable brother is available, the overseer himself may read or a capable sister may read.

Having the study groups scattered throughout the congregation territory makes it convenient both for us and for newly interested people in the neighborhood to attend. We should make every effort to bring others with us to the meeting so that they can get a taste of the spiritually upbuilding discussions and the warm association that we enjoy.

In addition to being a place for group study, the Congregation Book Study location may be a meeting place for field service. Here the group may meet at convenient times before going out into the field. By cooperating in all these arrangements, book study groups work together for the twofold purpose of study and service.

MEETINGS FOR FIELD SERVICE

At various times during the week, groups of Jehovah's Witnesses may briefly assemble in preparation for going out in the field ministry. Discussion of a Bible text—preferably the daily text if it is field service related—suggestions for dealing with situations likely to be encountered in the field, or points from *Our Kingdom Ministry* are usually considered at these meetings. Field service arrangements are made, and one of the group leads in prayer. The group is then ready to go into the field. Such meetings provide practical instruction and real encouragement for those going out in the witness work. Arrangements can be made at this meeting to help newer ones or others who may need assistance in the preaching work. Such meetings last from 10 to 15 minutes.

MEETING ARRANGEMENTS AT NEW OR SMALL CONGREGATIONS

As more become disciples, the number of congregations also increases. Whether a new congregation is formed from an already existing congregation or is made up of publishers in an isolated area, it must consist of baptized publishers and others who recognize the faithful and discreet slave class and desire to work under its direction. The circuit overseer usually submits the application for a new congregation. In some cases, small groups may find it more advantageous to be associated with the nearest congregation.

At times, small congregations may be composed entirely of sisters. When such is the case, a sister who prays in the congregation or conducts meetings does so with her head properly covered, in harmony with the Scriptural arrangement. (1 Cor. 11:3-16) In most cases, they remain seated, facing the group. None of the sisters give actual discourses at meetings. They read and comment on the material provided by Jehovah's Witnesses, or for variety, they may cover it in discussions or demonstrations.

In a newly formed congregation, brothers who qualify for appointment as elders or ministerial servants will be recommended to the branch office. If no one qualifies, as in the case of a group made up entirely of sisters, the branch office will designate one of the sisters to care for correspondence with the office and to carry on meetings. In time, when brothers qualify for appointment, they will care for these responsibilities.

SPECIAL ASSEMBLY DAYS AND CIRCUIT ASSEMBLIES

Meetings of Jehovah's servants may range in size from small gatherings of just two or three individuals to large assemblies of many thousands. Each year arrangements are made for congregations assigned to the same circuit to assemble together for a one-day special assembly day and a two-day circuit assembly. These joyous occasions afford everyone opportunities to "widen out" in Christian association. (2 Cor. 6:11-13) With a special need in mind, "the faithful and discreet slave" prepares the Scriptural themes and various parts of these programs.

The information is presented by means of a variety of methods, such as discourses, discussions, demonstrations, reenactments, and interviews. The programs usually feature parts that deal with local situations or counsel that specifically applies to the particular circuit. Such timely instruction builds up all who attend.

At special assembly days and circuit assemblies, opportunity is provided for new disciples to get baptized in symbol of their dedication to Jehovah. All are encouraged by the reports and experiences related concerning the work of preaching the good news.

DISTRICT CONVENTIONS

Once each year, larger gatherings are held by Jehovah's Witnesses. These are usually organized as three-day district conventions, combining congregations from a number of circuits. However, smaller branches may find it more practical and convenient for all congregations under the branch to assemble in one place. Arrangements for these gatherings in some lands may vary according to circumstances or on the basis of direction from the Governing Body. National conventions are also organized. Periodically, international conventions around the world may be attended by tens of thousands of Witnesses from a number of different lands. Over the years, many people have learned about the good news because of the publicity given to these large gatherings of Jehovah's Witnesses.

District, national, and international conventions are joyous occasions of united worship for Jehovah's dedicated people. Such conventions have provided the setting for revealing increased light on the truth, for releasing new publications for personal and congregational study and use in the field ministry, and for having baptisms. Jehovah's Witnesses consider district conventions to be of particular importance in promoting spiritual growth and in reviewing progress in fulfilling the Christian commission to preach the good news. In some smaller branches, the district convention may actually be a national convention. The larger conventions give evidence that Jehovah's people indeed form an international brotherhood of dedicated Christians bearing the identifying mark of disciples of Jesus Christ.—John 13:35.

By attending local congregation meetings as well as the larger assemblies and conventions of Jehovah's people, we are strengthened to do Jehovah's will and are protected against worldly influences that could undermine our Christian faith. We can all be thankful that Jehovah has provided these periods of spiritual refreshment for his dedicated people in this time of the end.

THE LORD'S EVENING MEAL

Once each year on the anniversary of the death of Jesus Christ, all congregations of Jehovah's Witnesses observe the Memorial of Christ's death, or the Lord's Evening Meal. (1 Cor. 11:20, 23, 24) This is the most important meeting of the year for Jehovah's people. We are specifically commanded to observe this Memorial.—Luke 22:19.

The date of the Memorial corresponds with the date of the Passover, which is clearly marked in the Bible. (Ex. 12:2, 6; Matt. 26:17, 20, 26) The Passover was the annual commemoration of the Exodus of the Israelites from Egypt in the year 1513 B.C.E. At that time Jehovah marked the 14th day of their first lunar month as the date for them to eat the Passover lamb and to leave their captivity in Egypt. (Ex. 12:1-51) The date is determined by counting 14 days from the new moon nearest the spring equinox as visible in Jerusalem. Generally, the Memorial observance each year falls on the date of the first full moon following the spring equinox.

Matthew 26:26-28 outlines in Jesus' own words the way the Memorial is observed. It is, not a ritual with mystical overtones, but a symbolic meal that is shared by those who have been called to be joint heirs with Jesus Christ in his heavenly Kingdom. (Luke 22:28-30) All other dedicated Christians and interested people are encouraged to attend the Lord's Evening Meal as observers. By their attendance they show their appreciation for the provision Jehovah God has made for the benefit of all mankind through his Son, Jesus Christ. Jehovah's Witnesses view the Memorial as a special event and make every effort to be in attendance each year.

In the first part of the year, usually near Memorial time, a special public talk is given in the congregations of Jehovah's Witnesses. They endeavor to invite all interested ones to attend. The talk provides a timely message for those who want to be pleasing to God and is designed to stimulate further interest in Bible study.

Jehovah's Witnesses joyfully anticipate occasions for assembling together at meetings, where we "consider one another to incite to love and fine works." (Heb. 10:24) "The faithful and discreet slave" is alert to provide such meetings according to our spiritual needs. All of Jehovah's servants as well as interested people are urged to take full advantage of the arrangements for regularly assembling together. By showing due appreciation for Jehovah's provisions through his organization, God's servants are bound together in unity.

CHAPTER 8

MINISTERS OF THE GOOD NEWS

IN SENDING forth his Son, Jehovah gave us a perfect model to follow. (1 Pet. 2:21) When anyone becomes his follower, Jesus helps that person to preach the good news as one of God's ministers. Indicating that this would be spiritually refreshing, Jesus said: "Come to me, all you who are toiling and loaded down, and I will refresh you. Take my yoke upon you and *learn from me* ["become my disciples," ftn.], for I am mild-tempered and lowly in heart, and you will find refreshment for your souls." (Matt. 11:28, 29) His promise has not failed any who have responded to that invitation!

As God's Chief Minister, Jesus called certain individuals to come and be his followers. (Matt. 9:9; John 1:43) He trained them in the ministry and sent them forth to do the same work he was doing. (Matt. 10:1–11:1; 20:28; Luke 4:43) Later he sent forth 70 others to share in declaring the good news concerning God's Kingdom. (Luke 10:1, 8-11) When Jesus sent his disciples forth, he said to them: "He that listens to you listens to me too. And he that disregards you disregards me too. Moreover, he that disregards me disregards also him that sent me forth." (Luke 10:16) In this way Jesus stressed the serious responsibility that was laid upon the disciples. They were to represent the Most High God! It would be the same with all others who respond to Jesus' invitation to "come be [his] follower," even down to this day. (Luke 18:22) All who respond have a divine commission to preach the good news of the Kingdom and to make disciples. —Matt. 24:14; 28:19, 20.

Having come to Jesus, therefore, in response to his invitation to follow him, we have been blessed with knowledge of Jehovah God and of Jesus Christ. (John 17:3) We have been taught Jehovah's ways. With his help we have been able to make our mind over, change our personality, and harmonize our daily conduct with Jehovah's righteous standards. (Rom. 12:1, 2; Eph. 4:22-24; Col. 3:9, 10) Our heartfelt appreciation has moved us to dedicate ourselves to Jehovah and to symbolize that by baptism in water. Baptism constitutes our ordination as ministers.

Always keep in mind that service to God must be rendered with clean hands and out of a pure heart. (Ps. 24:3, 4; Isa. 52:11; 2 Cor. 6:14–7:1) Through faith in Jesus Christ, we have gained a clean conscience and freeness of speech. (Heb. 10:19-23, 35, 36; Rev. 7: 9, 10, 14) The apostle Paul admonished Christians to do all things for God's glory, so as not to be stumbling others. Also, the apostle Peter pointed out the value of exemplary godly conduct in winning unbelievers over to the truth. (1 Cor. 10:31, 33; 1 Pet. 3:1) How can you help someone qualify to become a minister of the good news?

NEW PUBLISHERS

From the time you begin conducting a home Bible study with an interested person, encourage him to speak to others about what he is learning from the Bible. He could be urged to speak with relatives, friends, work associates, and others on an informal basis. This is an important step in teaching new ones to be followers of Jesus Christ as ministers of the good news. (Matt. 9:9; Luke 6:40) As the new one grows spiritually and becomes adept at informal witnessing, he will no doubt express a desire to have a share in the public ministry with the congregation.

MEETING THE REQUIREMENTS

Before inviting a person to accompany you in the field ministry for the first time and before you suggest that he report any field service to the congregation, there are certain qualifications he should meet. When a person accompanies us in the field ministry, he identifies himself publicly with the congregation of Jehovah's people, so it is understood that he has already brought his life into harmony with Jehovah's righteous standards and can be an unbaptized publisher in the congregation.

Very likely, as you study with a person and discuss Bible principles with him, you will become aware of his circumstances. You may observe that he is living in harmony with the information he has learned from studying the Bible. But there are some aspects of the student's life that the elders will want to discuss with him and you together before you invite him to accompany you in the field service and to share in publicly witnessing to others.

The presiding overseer will arrange to have two elders (one being a member of the Congregation Service Committee) discuss this matter with you and the Bible student. They will consider the following points:

- Do the person's expressions show that he believes that the Bible is the inspired Word of God? (2 Tim. 3:16)

- Does he know and believe the basic teachings of the Scriptures so that when asked questions, he will answer in harmony with the Bible and not according to false religious teachings or his own ideas? (Matt. 7:21-23; 2 Tim. 2:15)
- Is he heeding the Bible's command to associate with Jehovah's people at congregation meetings if he physically and circumstantially can? (Ps. 122:1; Heb. 10:24, 25)
- Does he know what the Bible teaches about fornication, adultery, polygamy, and homosexuality, and is he living in harmony with such teachings? If the person is living with one of the opposite sex, are they properly married? (Matt. 19:9; 1 Cor. 6:9, 10; 1 Tim. 3:2, 12; Heb. 13:4)
- Does he heed the Bible's prohibition of drunkenness? (Eph. 5:18; 1 Pet. 4:3, 4) Is he free from all nonmedical use of addictive or mind-altering natural or synthetic substances? (2 Cor. 7:1)
- Does he see the value of avoiding unwholesome association? (1 Cor. 15:33)
- Has he definitely broken off membership in all false religious organizations with which he may have been affiliated, and has he ceased attending their meetings and supporting or sharing in their activities? (2 Cor. 6:14-18; Rev. 18:4)
- Is he free from all involvement in the political affairs of the world? (John 6:15; 15:19; Jas. 1:27)
- Does he believe and live in harmony with what the Bible says at Isaiah 2:4 about the affairs of the nations?
- Does he really want to be one of Jehovah's Witnesses? (Ps. 110:3)

If the elders are not sure how the student feels about some of these matters, they should invite him to look up the scriptures here cited and comment on them in order to see the significance of what they say. It is important that he understand that those who share with Jehovah's Witnesses in their preaching activity must be leading a life that harmonizes with these Scriptural requirements. His expressions will help the elders determine whether he knows what is expected of him and whether he is qualified to a reasonable degree to begin participating in the field ministry.

If he is qualified, the elders can warmly welcome the individual as one who desires to become an active associate of Jehovah's Witnesses. (Rom. 15:7) He should be encouraged to begin sharing in the field ministry as soon as possible and to turn in a field service report at the end of the month. The elders can explain that when a Bible student qualifies as an unbaptized publisher and reports field service for the first time, a *Congregation's Publisher Record* card is made out in his name and included in the congregation file. They can assure him that all the elders take an interest in the field service reports that are turned in each month.

Getting better acquainted with the new publisher and showing a personal interest in what he has accomplished can have a fine influence on the individual. It may move him to make even greater efforts to serve Jehovah and to turn in field service reports regularly each month.—Phil. 2:4; Heb. 13:2.

Once the elders determine that the Bible student qualifies to engage in the field ministry, he is eligible to receive his own copy of *Organized to Do Jehovah's Will*. After he reports field service for the first time, a brief announcement should be made to the congregation that he is a new unbaptized publisher.

HELPING YOUNG PEOPLE

Young children may also qualify as publishers of the good news. Jesus received young children to himself and blessed them. (Matt. 19:13-15; 21:15, 16) Although primarily parents are responsible for their own children, others in the congregation may wish to help young ones who are motivated from the heart to share in the Kingdom-preaching work. If you are a parent, your fine example in the field ministry will do much to encourage your children to be zealous in their service to God. When a child is exemplary in his conduct and is moved from the heart to make a personal expression of his faith by speaking to others about the good news, what further help can be given?

It would be appropriate for the parent to approach one of the elders on the Congregation Service Committee to discuss whether the child is qualified to become a publisher. The presiding overseer will arrange to have two elders (one being a member of the Congregation Service Committee) meet with the child and his parent(s). If the child has a basic knowledge of Bible truth and gives evidence of *wanting* to share in Kingdom service, this would indicate good progress has been made. After considering these and other factors similar to those that apply to adults, the two elders can determine whether the child may be recognized as an unbaptized publisher.—Luke 6:45; Rom. 10:10.

DEDICATION AND BAPTISM

If you have taken in accurate knowledge and have shown love for God by conforming your life to divine requirements and by sharing in the field ministry, you need to solidify your personal relationship with Jehovah. How? By making a dedication to him in prayer and then symbolizing this by water baptism. —Matt. 28:19, 20.

Dedication signifies a setting apart for a sacred purpose. To make a dedication to God means to approach him in prayer and solemnly to promise to use your life to serve him and to walk in his ways faithfully, giving him exclusive devotion forever. (Deut. 5:9) In this way you dedicate yourself to God. This is a personal, private matter. No one else can do it for you.

However, you must do more than privately tell Jehovah that you want to belong to him. You need to show others that you have made a dedication to God. You make it known by getting baptized in water, just as Jesus did. (1 Pet. 2:21; 3:21) If you have made up your mind to serve Jehovah and want to get baptized, what should you do? You should make your desire known to the presiding overseer of the congregation of Jehovah's Witnesses with which you are associating. He will arrange for several elders to hold discussions with you to make sure that you meet the divine requirements for baptism. For further information, please review "A Message to the Unbaptized Publisher," found on pages 180-2 of this publication, and "Questions for Those Desiring to Be Baptized," found on pages 182-215.

REPORTING ON THE PROGRESS OF THE MINISTRY

Reports on the worldwide expansion of pure worship have been a source of genuine encouragement for Jehovah's people over the years. From the time Jesus first told his disciples that the good news would be preached throughout all the earth, true Christians have been vitally concerned with knowing how this would be accomplished.—Matt. 28:19, 20; Mark 13:10; Acts 1:8.

Early followers of Jesus Christ took an interest in reports of progress in the preaching work. (Mark 6:30) The Bible book of Acts tells us that there were about 120 persons present when holy spirit was poured out on the disciples at Pentecost. Soon the number of disciples grew to 3,000 and then to 5,000. The encouraging report was made that "Jehovah continued to join to them daily those being saved" and that "a great crowd of priests began to be obedient to the faith." (Acts 1:15; 2:5-11, 41, 47; 4:4; 6:7) What fine encouragement the news of these increases must have brought to the disciples! How these exciting reports must have impelled them to move ahead with their divinely commissioned work, in spite of severe persecution spearheaded by the Jewish religious leaders!

About 60-61 C.E., Paul reported in his letter to the Colossians that the good news was "bearing fruit and increasing in all the world" and had been "preached in all creation that is under heaven." (Col. 1:5, 6, 23) The early Christians had been obedient to the Word, and holy spirit had empowered them to accomplish a worldwide preaching work before the end of the Jewish system of things in 70 C.E. A seemingly impossible task had been completed. How encouraging it was for those faithful Christian workers to hear reports of what was being accomplished!

In like manner, Jehovah's modern-day organization endeavors to keep precise records of the work being done in fulfillment of Matthew 24:14, which says: "This good news of the kingdom will be preached in all the inhabited earth for a witness to all the nations; and then the end will come." As dedicated servants of God, we have an urgent work to do. We must be personally interested in seeing that the ministry is accomplished thoroughly before the end comes. Jehovah will see to it that this work is completed, and if we have a share, we will receive Jehovah's smile of approval.

YOUR PERSONAL FIELD SERVICE REPORT

What exactly are we to report? The *Field Service Report* slip provided by the organization indicates what information is to be included, but perhaps the following general comments, along with additional clarifications that are set out from time to time in *Our Kingdom Ministry,* will prove to be helpful.

In the columns titled "Books," "Booklets & Brochures," and "Individual Magazines," list the total number of any of these publications that you placed with people who are not dedicated, baptized Witnesses.

In reporting "Return Visits," count the total number of return calls made for the purpose of further stimulating interest previously shown by someone who is not a dedicated, baptized Witness. In order to count a return visit, you need to contact the particular individual who previously showed interest. When you conduct a home Bible study with an inactive brother or sister at the direction of a member of the Congregation Service Committee, you should report a return visit. You may also report return visits for studies conducted with a newly baptized person who needs temporary assistance. A return visit can be made not only by calling on someone at home but also by writing a letter, making a telephone call, or delivering some literature, such as the latest issue of a magazine. Each time a home Bible study is conducted, it should be counted as a return visit.

Although Bible studies are usually conducted each week, they are reported only once each month. In lands where the *Study Report* slip is used, publishers should report each Bible study conducted during the month with people who are not dedicated, baptized Witnesses or with others as explained in the following paragraph. After filling out each slip completely and accurately, write the total number of different Bible studies in the box at the lower right-hand corner of your *Field Service Report* slip. The number you indicate on the *Field Service Report* slip and the number of *Study Report* slips you turn in should be the same.

It is important to submit an accurate report of "Hours of Field Service." Basically, this is the time you spend participating in the house-to-house ministry, engaging in street witnessing, making return visits, conducting Bible studies, or otherwise witnessing informally or publicly to people who are not dedicated and baptized Witnesses. You may also count a Bible study that you conduct with an inactive brother or sister at the direction of a member of the Congregation Service Committee. Additionally, you may continue reporting time used in conducting a study with a newly baptized person who needs temporary spiritual help. If for some reason two publishers are working together, both may count the time if both share in giving a witness. There are essential activities for which time is not counted, such as getting ready for field service, attending the meeting for field service, and traveling to and from the territory.

Your field service time should start when you begin your witness work and end when you finish your last call in each witnessing period. Time used for having refreshments or meals during a period of field service is not to be counted. Auxiliary, regular, and special pioneers as well as missionaries have hour requirements to meet. Congregation publishers are likewise encouraged to put Kingdom interests first and exert themselves in the ministry to accomplish all that they can in the field according to their individual circumstances. All of Jehovah's dedicated servants endeavor to be whole-souled in the ministry. (Col. 3:23) Those giving public talks may count the time spent delivering these, and a parent may count up to one hour each week when studying with his or her undedicated children.

Time spent in the field service should be reported in full hours. An exception to this is made when a publisher is very limited because of advanced age, is shut-in, is confined to a nursing home, or is otherwise incapacitated. Such a publisher may report field service in 15-minute increments rather than in full hours. Even if he gives a witness for just 15 minutes during a month, he should report this time so that he can continue to be counted as a regular Kingdom publisher. This arrangement also applies to a publisher who is temporarily limited, perhaps unable to move about during a month or so because of a serious illness or injury. This provision is made, however, only for those who are *very limited* in their activity. The Congregation Service Committee will determine whether a publisher qualifies for this arrangement.

CONGREGATION'S PUBLISHER RECORD CARD

Your individual field service report for each month is compiled and recorded on a *Congregation's Publisher Record* card, which is kept as a part of the congregation files. These cards are not personal property. If you move to another congregation, be sure to inform the elders. The secretary of your new congregation will request that your *Congregation's Publisher Record* card(s) be forwarded. If the secretary of your former congregation knows the name of the congregation to which you have relocated, he can take the initiative in sending the record card(s) along with a letter of introduction. Consequently, the elders of your new congregation will be in a better position to continue giving you needed spiritual assistance. If you are to be away from your congregation for a period of less than three months, please continue to send your field service reports regularly to your home congregation.

WHY WE REPORT OUR FIELD SERVICE

Do you sometimes forget to turn in your field service report? No doubt all of us need occasional reminders. But if we cultivate the right attitude toward reporting our field ministry and if we understand why doing so is important, it may become easier for us to remember to report our field service properly.

Some have asked: "Since Jehovah knows what I am doing in his service, why do I need to put in a report to the congregation?" True, Jehovah knows what we are doing, and he is able to judge whether our service is whole-souled or just a token of what we are really able to do. Remember, however, that Jehovah recorded the number of days that Noah spent in the ark and the number of years that the Israelites journeyed in the wilderness. God kept account of the number of those who were faithful as well as those who disobeyed. He recorded the progressive conquest of the land of Canaan and the accomplishments of the faithful judges of Israel. Yes, he recorded many details regarding the deeds and accomplishments of his servants. He inspired this written record of what took place, making clear to us his view of keeping accurate records.

Historical events recorded in the Bible demonstrate the exactness of reports and records kept by Jehovah's name people. In many cases, the full impact of the Bible account could not be conveyed without reporting the specific numbers. Consider the following examples: Genesis 46:27 and Exodus 12:37; Judges 7:7; 2 Kings 19:35; 2 Chronicles 14:9-13; John 6:10; 21:11; Acts 2:41; 19:19.

There are a number of reasons why we report our field service today. Although these reports obviously do not include all that we do in serving Jehovah, what is reported serves a practical purpose in helping all within Jehovah's organization, including the local elders.

At times, reports may indicate that particular attention needs to be given to certain aspects of our ministry. The figures may show that there has been progress in some activities but that publisher increase or growth in other areas has slowed down. It could be that encouragement is needed or that there are problems to be resolved. Responsible overseers will take note of reports and endeavor to rectify any condition that may be hindering the progress of individuals or of the congregation as a whole.

Also, reports are beneficial organizationally in determining just where there is a greater need for workers in the field. What areas are more productive? Where is little progress being made? What publications are needed to help people learn the truth? Reports enable the organization to project literature needs for different areas of the world and then to keep ahead of the need so that there is not a shortage of Bibles or Bible literature for use in the preaching work.

For most of us, reports mean encouragement. Are we not thrilled when we hear about the work our brothers are doing in preaching the good news worldwide? Reports of increases in the number of publishers help us to get an overall view of the expansion of Jehovah's organization. Individual experiences warm our hearts and fill us with zeal, moving us to have a fuller share in the preaching work. (Acts 15:3) So our cooperation with the congregation in turning in field service reports is important and shows our concern for the brothers everywhere. In this small way, we demonstrate our submission to Jehovah's organizational arrangement.—Matt. 24:45-47.

SETTING PERSONAL GOALS

There is no reason for us to compare our field service with that of another person. (Gal. 5:26; 6:4) Individual circumstances vary greatly, making it unwise for us to make such comparisons. On the other hand, we can derive much benefit from setting realistic personal goals. These can give us a valuable basis for measuring our own progress in the ministry. Also, if we set our personal goals according to our individual circumstances, attaining these goals can give us the satisfaction that comes with accomplishment.

SHARE IN A FINAL REPORT

Regarding a symbolic work that was prophetic of the preaching work we are doing today, we are told that a report was made when the work was finished. In prophetic vision, Ezekiel saw six men with smashing weapons in their hands coming forth to execute judgment upon apostate Jerusalem. But he also saw a seventh man come forth. This one had a secretary's inkhorn with him, and he was told: "Pass through the midst of the city, through the midst of Jerusalem, and you must put a mark on the foreheads of the men that are sighing and groaning over all the detestable things that are being done in the midst of it." After finishing his work of marking those who were to be saved from execution by the men with the smashing weapons, the man with the secretary's inkhorn returned to make a report, saying: "I have done just as you have commanded me."—Ezek. 9:1-11.

We do not know what final report Jehovah will request regarding the grand preaching work accomplished in fulfillment of Matthew 24:14. However, we can demonstrate our appreciation for the small part we are allowed to have in the ministry by conscientiously reporting our field service regularly each month. All publishers of the good news should report their service activity promptly at the end of each month. Doing so will be greatly appreciated by the brothers who are assigned to compile the congregation field service report for mailing to the branch office.

It is obvious that Jehovah is now, indeed, speeding up the ingathering of those people he will protect through "the great tribulation." We are living in the time of fulfillment of Isaiah's prophecy in this regard: "The little one himself will become a thousand, and the small one a mighty nation. I myself, Jehovah, shall speed it up in its own time." (Rev. 7:9, 14; Isa. 60:22) As part of the worldwide association of those entrusted with the ministry, we want to be able to report, as did the visionary man with the secretary's inkhorn: "I have done just as you have commanded me."

CHAPTER 9

METHODS OF PREACHING THE GOOD NEWS

JESUS CHRIST took very seriously his commission as Jehovah's sent-forth one. As a vigorous proclaimer of the good news of God's Kingdom, he set an example for his followers. He took the initiative to go out among the people, speaking and teaching in their homes and in public places. (Matt. 9:35; Luke 8:1) Jesus spoke with individuals, taught his disciples privately, and addressed groups numbering into the thousands. (Matt. 13:36; Mark 4:10-13; 6:35-44; John 3:2-21) He took advantage of every appropriate occasion to speak words of encouragement and hope. (Luke 4:16-19) He did not pass up opportunities to witness, even when he was in need of rest and refreshment. (Mark 6:30-34; John 4:4-34) When we read the inspired accounts of Jesus' ministry, are we not impelled to imitate his example? Certainly we are, just as the apostles were.—Matt. 4:19, 20; Luke 5:27, 28; John 1:43-45.

Consider the opportunities that are open to Christians today to share in the work initiated by Jesus Christ nearly 2,000 years ago.

PREACHING FROM HOUSE TO HOUSE

Jehovah's modern-day Witnesses recognize the value of preaching the good news systematically from house to house. They have used this method of reaching people with the Kingdom message so extensively that it has virtually become their trademark. The good results obtained give evidence of Jehovah's approval and blessing. Also, the wisdom of using this method to reach millions of people effectively during a short period of time has been confirmed by the gratifying results. (Matt. 11:19; 24:14) This approach has proved to be a practical way for us to demonstrate love for Jehovah and for our neighbors.—Matt. 22:34-40.

House-to-house preaching is not a modern innovation of Jehovah's Witnesses. It was firmly established in the days of the apostles. Outstandingly, the apostle Paul refers to his teaching in the homes of people. Describing his ministry to the overseers in Ephesus, he said: "From the first day that I stepped into the district of Asia I . . . did not hold back from telling you any of the things that were profitable nor from teaching you publicly and from house to house." In this and other ways, he "thoroughly bore witness both to Jews and to Greeks about repentance toward God and faith in our Lord Jesus." (Acts 20:18, 20, 21) At that time, there was an urgent need to reach all the people with the good news, since the Roman emperors encouraged idolatry and many peoples were "given to the fear of the deities." There was a pressing need to seek "the God that made the world and all the things in it," the One who was then "telling mankind that they should all everywhere repent."—Acts 17:22-31.

Today the need to reach people with the good news is even more urgent. The end of the present wicked system of things is rapidly approaching. Life itself hangs in the balance for all mankind. So there is need for intensive effort on our part now, before the end comes. Seeing this need, we are moved to increase our efforts in the house-to-house ministry, realizing that no better way has been found than this time-tested method of searching for those who are hungering for the truth. It is as effective today as it was in the days of Jesus and the apostles. It is a satisfying way for us to have a share in the ministry. —Mark 13:10.

According to your personal circumstances, are you having a full share in the house-to-house ministry? If you are taking advantage of every opportunity to do so, we know that you are reaping a rich reward of joy and personal satisfaction in your service to God. (Ezek. 9:11; Acts 20:35) The house-to-house ministry may not be easy for you. You may have physical limitations, or you may be assigned to work in territory where many people are not inclined to listen. There may even be governmental restrictions with which to cope. Because of your personality makeup, you may find it very difficult to initiate conversations with total strangers and must therefore overcome a measure of anxiety each time you engage in the house-to-house ministry. Do not be discouraged. (Ex. 4:10-12) Your circumstances are not unlike those of your brothers in many other places.

Jesus promised his disciples that he would be with them "all the days until the conclusion of the system of things." (Matt. 28:20) That promise encourages his disciples today and fortifies them in the disciple-making work. We must take courage and have confidence like that expressed by Paul, as found at Philippians 4:13. He said: "For all things I have the strength by virtue of him who imparts power to me." Take full advantage of congregation arrangements made each week for engaging in house-to-house witnessing. By working with others, you will receive encouragement and personal assistance to talk effectively with people and to present Bible literature. Pray for greater faith to overcome whatever obstacles you may face, and exert yourself vigorously as a preacher of the good news.—Luke 17:5.

As you speak to others about the good news, you will have opportunities to give a reason for your hope, and your own hope will be made firm. (1 Pet. 3:15) You will become more and more aware of the sharp contrast between those who have the Kingdom hope and those who are without hope. Finding those deserving of the Kingdom message and noting the reactions of those who are not will enable you personally to experience what Jesus told his disciples, as recorded at Matthew 10:11-14. You will have the satisfaction of knowing that you have been obedient to Jesus' command to "let your light shine," and you may even be privileged to help others to come to a knowledge of the truth that leads to everlasting life.—Matt. 5:16; John 17:3; 1 Tim. 4:16.

Arrangements are made for house-to-house activity on weekends as well as during the week. In areas where it is very difficult to find people at home during the day, some congregations arrange for evening witnessing. They have found that people are more inclined to receive visitors in the late afternoon or early evening hours than in the morning. Also, there are other features of the ministry that may be effective in your area.

SEARCHING OUT DESERVING ONES

Jesus instructed his disciples to "search out" deserving ones. (Matt. 10:11) His search for those favorably disposed was not limited to the house-to-house ministry. Indeed, he gave a witness on every appropriate occasion, both formal and informal. (Luke 8:1; John 4:7-15) The apostles also witnessed to people at a variety of locations.—Acts 17:17; 28: 16, 23, 30, 31.

Likewise today, our objective is to reach *everyone* possible with the Kingdom message. This means imitating Jesus and his disciples in their approach to the disciple-making work as well as keeping abreast of the changing times and the varying circumstances of the people in our territory.—1 Cor. 7:31.

In addition to preaching from house to house, we must search for people elsewhere. Publishers have been successful in calling on people at places of business. Street witnessing has proved very effective in many countries, as has witnessing in parks, in parking lots, on public transportation, or wherever people can be found. As a result, individuals who are not at home when publishers call may be contacted with the good news.

Presenting *The Watchtower* and *Awake!* is an effective way to witness to people. This can be done in a kind and tactful manner by approaching people with a timely subject discussed in one of the magazines. Other literature may also be offered to interested people, and arrangements may then be made to call on them at their homes. Periodically, *Our Kingdom Ministry* offers suggestions regarding this, encouraging us to share in various features of the ministry. You may find witnessing to people in public places an enjoyable way to expand your ministry.

However, sounding a warning and proclaiming the good news are not all that is involved in the work assigned to Christians today. If you are to succeed in helping others embrace the truth that leads to life, you need to make repeated calls on interested ones so that they can progress toward becoming mature Christians.

MAKING RETURN VISITS

Jesus said to his followers: "You will be witnesses of me . . . to the most distant part of the earth." (Acts 1:8) But he also told them: "Go therefore and make disciples of people of all the nations, . . . teaching them to observe all the things I have commanded you." (Matt. 28:19, 20) Making return visits can be a source of joy in Jehovah's service. People who expressed interest in the good news when you first called on them will likely be happy to receive you again. By sharing additional Bible information with them, you may be able to strengthen their faith in God and help them to become aware of their spiritual need. (Matt. 5:3) If you arrange to make the return visit at a convenient time and prepare well, you may be able to start a home Bible study. Doing so will usually be your objective in making return visits. We not only 'plant' the seed of truth but also 'water' it.—1 Cor. 3:6.

Making return visits may present a challenge for some. Perhaps you have become quite proficient in making a brief presentation of the good news from house to house, and you enjoy that particular feature of the ministry. But when you think of returning to engage the householder in a more detailed discussion of the Bible, the challenge may seem overwhelming. You need not feel that way. Very likely on your first call, you placed some Bible literature with the interested person. Why not discuss information contained in that publication? You can prepare for that ahead of time. If you do not feel entirely qualified, arrange to take along a more experienced publisher to help you.

Jehovah's organization provides the personal assistance you need to become effective in making return visits. Be sure that you take full advantage of opportunities to improve your own knowledge and understanding of the Scriptures. Trust in Jehovah, and accept the assistance of experienced brothers and sisters. If you do, you will improve in your ability to make effective return visits, and your joy in service will increase accordingly.

CONDUCTING HOME BIBLE STUDIES

When speaking to a man who was interested in the message of God's Word, the evangelizer Philip asked him: "Do you actually know what you are reading?" The man responded: "Really, how could I ever do so, unless someone guided me?" The Bible account in Acts chapter 8 then tells us that starting with the scripture the man had been reading, Philip "declared to him the good news about Jesus." (Acts 8: 26-36) We do not know how much time Philip spent with the man, but Philip explained the good news to the point that the man became a believer and requested water baptism. He became a disciple of Jesus Christ.

An interested person we find today may not be familiar with the Bible, so it may require a number of return visits and a detailed study over a period of weeks, months, or even a year or more before he is able to manifest faith and qualify for baptism. But your patient and loving assistance in helping honesthearted ones become disciples has its own reward, even as Jesus said: "There is more happiness in giving than there is in receiving."—Acts 20:35.

You will no doubt find it easier to conduct a home Bible study using one of the publications of Jehovah's Witnesses that is especially designed for that purpose. By following the example of the one who studied with you or by receiving help from other capable teachers in the congregation, you may be able to improve in your ability to conduct productive studies, helping others to become disciples of Jesus Christ.

If you need assistance in starting and conducting a home Bible study, feel free to speak with one of the overseers or with a fellow Witness who is effective in the Bible study work. You can receive help to put into practice the suggestions that have appeared in *Our Kingdom Ministry* and have been demonstrated at the Service Meeting. Relying on Jehovah and making your desire a matter of prayer will bring results. (1 John 3:22) So share in making disciples, and if at all possible, make it your aim to conduct at least one home Bible study regularly in addition to any study that you may conduct with your family. By conducting Bible studies, you will increase your joy in the ministry.

DIRECTING INTERESTED ONES TO JEHOVAH'S ORGANIZATION

When we conduct Bible studies and help people become disciples of Jesus Christ, they come to know Jehovah God and are brought into the congregation. Congregations are organized theocratically to do Jehovah's will. Bible students will make spiritual progress and grow to maturity if we help them to recognize Jehovah's organization and cooperate with it. It is important to teach them how.

To accomplish this, you can use videos and brochures that have been specifically prepared for this purpose. Some of the information found in Chapter 4 of this publication may also be helpful.

From the very beginning of your Bible discussions with interested people, help them to see that Jehovah is using an organization to get his work done on earth today. Point out the value of the Bible study aids used by Jehovah's Witnesses, and explain how they are produced and distributed worldwide by volunteer workers who are dedicated to God. Invite your Bible students to accompany you to the Congregation Book Study. Introduce them to the brothers and sisters there, and explain how meetings at the Kingdom Hall are conducted. Encourage them to attend. Help them to get acquainted with other Witnesses at circuit assemblies and district conventions. On these and other occasions, let new ones observe for themselves how Jehovah's servants display the identifying mark of true Christians, love. (John 13:35) As interested people grow in appreciation for Jehovah's organization, they will make greater advancement in getting to know Jehovah.

USING BIBLE LITERATURE

The early Christians became zealous publishers of the Word of God. They made copies of the Scriptures for their personal use and for congregation study. They recommended God's Word of truth to others. Their handwritten copies were few in number and highly treasured. (Col. 4:16; 2 Tim. 2:15; 3: 14-17; 4:13; 1 Pet. 1:1) Using modern printing methods today, Jehovah's Witnesses publish millions of Bibles and hundreds of millions of Bible study aids—such as tracts, brochures, books, and magazines—in scores of languages.

As you share the good news with others, be sure to make good use of the numerous Bible study aids provided by "the faithful and discreet slave." (Matt. 24:45) *Our Kingdom Ministry* announces which publications are to be featured in public witnessing during each month. You also have opportunity to share regularly in distributing magazines at different times each month, including magazine days.

Although the primary concern of 'the faithful slave' has been to provide spiritual food at the proper time for the household of God, that "slave" has reflected the generosity of Jehovah God in providing an abundance of spiritual food for anyone who hungers for knowledge of him. Knowing how much you have personally benefited from reading and studying the publications of Jehovah's Witnesses, you will no doubt want to share with others the things you have learned. (Heb. 13:15, 16) Using those publications, even new ones can accomplish much good in preaching the good news.

INFORMAL WITNESSING

Jesus told those who were paying attention to his word: "You are the light of the world. . . . Let your light shine before men, that they may see your fine works and give glory to your Father who is in the heavens." (Matt. 5:14-16) These disciples should reflect God's ways by imitating Jesus Christ, who also said: "I am the light of the world." Jesus set the example for Christians in letting "the light of life" shine for the benefit of all who would listen.—John 8:12.

The apostle Paul likewise set an example for us to follow. (1 Cor. 4:16; 11:1) While in Athens, he witnessed every day in the marketplace to those who happened to be on hand. (Acts 17:17) The Christians in Philippi followed his example, and he addressed them as 'illuminators in the world, shining among a crooked and twisted generation.' (Phil. 2:15) We today can also let the Kingdom truth shine forth by our words and actions whenever there is an opportunity for us to tell others about the good news. True, our good example as honest and upright people may in itself draw attention to the fact that we are different from the majority of mankind. However, if we open our mouth to speak the good news to those who see our fine example, they will get to know *why* we are different from the rest.

Many of Jehovah's Witnesses present the good news to people whom they meet daily in their secular work, at school, or while going about their normal affairs of life. When on a journey, we may have the opportunity to talk with fellow travelers. Individually, we must be alert to opportunities to turn ordinary conversation into a witness and be prepared to speak with others on every appropriate occasion.

We will be encouraged to share the good news with others if we keep in mind that whenever we do so, we are praising our Creator and bringing honor to his name. At the same time, we may be able to help honesthearted ones come to know Jehovah so that they too can serve him and gain the hope of life that comes through faith in Jesus Christ. All of this is sacred service, and it is pleasing to God.—Heb. 12:28; Rev. 7:9, 10.

TERRITORY

It is Jehovah's purpose to have the Kingdom message preached worldwide in both city and rural areas in an orderly manner. To this end, congregations as well as individuals who witness in isolated areas receive territory assignments from the branch office directing the work in their respective lands. (1 Cor. 14:40) This is consistent with the God-directed arrangement existing in the first century. (2 Cor. 10:13; Gal. 2:9) With the rapid expansion of the Kingdom work in these last days, duplication of effort is avoided when territory assignments are well organized. This affords opportunity for more people to hear the good news.

The overall arrangement for working congregation territory comes under the supervision of the service overseer. A ministerial servant may do the actual assigning of territory and keep the records up-to-date. Where territory is limited, the Congregation Book Study overseer usually holds the territory in which publishers in the group may share in field service.

If you are in a congregation where territory is plentiful, however, you may wish to have a territory of your own, perhaps one near where you live. Having a conveniently located personal territory will enable you to make the most of the time you can devote to field service. Also, you may wish to invite another publisher to work with you in your personal territory.

When such personal territory is available, you may approach the territory servant in your congregation and request one that has not already been assigned to someone else. You should keep the territory servant informed as to the coverage of that territory. As you work your personal territory, you will get acquainted with many people, and with patience, you may have the joy of helping some of them come to appreciate God's provision for salvation.

Of course, if you have a personal territory, it will be your responsibility to get in touch with as many people in that territory as you can. This will entail calling back where no one was at home and rendering spiritual assistance to those who show interest in the good news of the Kingdom. From time to time, *Our Kingdom Ministry* makes specific suggestions as to how territory can be worked thoroughly with the use of Bibles, books, magazines, brochures, tracts, handbills, and other provisions of "the faithful and discreet slave." It may be that some of the people in your territory, such as those living in gated communities or high-security buildings, will have to be reached by letter, by telephone, or by other means, such as street witnessing. The service overseer and your Congregation Book Study overseer can offer appropriate suggestions in accord with local conditions and individual circumstances.

When all those associated with the congregation cooperate, the territory can be worked in a thorough and effective manner. We can also avoid simultaneous coverage of the same area by two or more Witnesses, something that could confuse or irritate the householders. Thus we show consideration both for our brothers and for the people in the territory.

WITNESSING TO PEOPLE OF ALL LANGUAGES

All mankind needs to learn about Jehovah God, his Son, and the Kingdom. (Rev. 14:6, 7) We are interested in helping those in our territory who speak another language to call on the name of Jehovah for salvation and to put on the Christian personality. (Rom. 10:12, 13; Col. 3:10, 11) Yet, how can the various situations and challenges that arise in presenting the good news to such ones be handled in a loving and effective manner?

Christians should treat others as they themselves would like to be treated. (Matt. 7:12) Extending a warm welcome to those of another land or language reflects genuine personal interest. (Rom. 15:7) This mental disposition is vital as we preach the good news in immigrant communities, since it helps us to view others as God views them.—Acts 10:34, 35; 17:26.

When you meet a person in the territory who speaks a tongue that you do not understand, endeavor to find out which language he reads. Share with him the message found in the booklet *Good News for People of All Nations*. If a congregation or a group in that language is nearby, perhaps you can help the person get in touch with those brothers. It may be that a local publisher who knows the language would be able to follow up on the interest. Otherwise, let the householder know that you will try to obtain one of our publications in that language. Then check with the literature servant to see what publications are available in that particular language.

Some publishers have learned enough of a language to give a simple presentation. Others have accepted the challenge of studying with a person, using one of our publications printed in his language. If we use the pictures and have the person read the cited Scriptures, he will get some basic Bible understanding. There may even be a member of his family who knows enough of his language and the local language to serve as an interpreter.

Keeping in mind that our purpose is to make disciples, encourage the interested person to attend the meetings of the local congregation if none are held in the language that he understands. The Christian association itself can be upbuilding and will help him make further spiritual progress.

When a congregation territory includes a sizable immigrant community, the elders should organize the preaching work so that spiritual help can be given. It may be that the foreign-language population is widely scattered throughout the territories of two or more neighboring congregations. In such a case, the circuit overseer(s) will help elders follow the direction outlined by the branch office, thus enabling the congregations involved to cooperate in the preaching activity. Periodically, a public talk or *Watchtower* Study may be held to determine the extent of support for meetings in the foreign language.

A foreign-language group can be formed when the following requirements are met: (1) There are publishers or interested ones who adequately understand the good news in the foreign language, (2) a qualified elder or a ministerial servant is available to take the lead and conduct at least one weekly meeting, and (3) a body of elders is willing to sponsor the group. When these requirements have been met, the elders should inform the branch office so that the group can be formally recognized and given further instructions.

Generally, one of the first meetings that a group will hold each week is the Congregation Book Study. Later, the elders may approve of holding other meetings, such as the Public Meeting and the *Watchtower* Study. Student assignments on the Theocratic Ministry School may be presented in an auxiliary classroom if an elder or a ministerial servant conversant with the language can serve as the counselor. Meetings for field service may also be arranged for the group. The same theocratic direction applies for every language.

All in the group work under the oversight of the body of elders sponsoring the group. The elders will provide balanced direction and show initiative in caring for the needs of the group. When a circuit overseer works with the group during the week of his visit to the congregation that sponsors the group, he will provide the branch office with a brief report on its progress and any specific needs that exist. If all involved in working the foreign-language field apply Scriptural and theocratic direction, Jehovah's name will be glorified.—1 Cor. 1:10; 3:5, 6.

WORKING MULTILINGUAL TERRITORIES

In most metropolitan areas, the publishers of each congregation should concentrate on speaking to people of their own specific language group because territory assignments in multilingual areas are made according to language. In congregations working multilingual territory, the service overseers of the congregations involved can work out a mutually acceptable system of covering the territory and directing interested ones to the appropriate congregation. This is necessary, since publishers of different-language congregations may be working the same territory during the same morning or afternoon, and we do not want to "offer any hindrance to the good news about the Christ."—1 Cor. 9:12.

When participating in street witnessing and informal witnessing, publishers may carry literature in various languages. However, when going from house to house, they would normally offer literature in the language of their congregation. Keep in mind that territories in these areas are prepared according to language so that publishers placing literature can also direct the interested person to the congregation meetings held in the language that he understands best or prefers. (1 Cor. 14:9) By concentrating our ministry on people who understand or prefer the language of the congregation we attend, we can help more people gain salvation.

GROUP WITNESSING

Dedicated Christians have a personal responsibility to share the good news with others. There are many ways to do this, but most of us appreciate being able to go out in field service with others. (Luke 10:1) For this reason, congregations meet for field service on weekends as well as during the week. Holidays also provide fine opportunities for group witnessing, since many brothers have time off from work. Meetings for field service are scheduled for the convenience of the publishers. These may be held at the Kingdom Hall, at homes where Congregation Book Studies are conducted, or at other convenient and proper places.

At meetings for field service, arrangements can be made to give assistance to those who are newer or less experienced. Also, in some areas it may be advisable for two or more publishers to work together for other reasons. Those working together can always be helpful and encouraging to one another. Even if you are planning to work by yourself in the territory, meeting with the group can be encouraging for all concerned. Just knowing that others are out in service working in the same general area can give you confidence.

May all of us follow the pattern set by Jesus and the apostles! We can be certain of Jehovah's blessing on our endeavors to have a full share in the vital work of preaching this good news of the Kingdom. —Luke 9:57-62.

CHAPTER 10

WAYS TO EXPAND YOUR MINISTRY

WHEN the time came for Jesus to send his disciples out as Kingdom preachers, he said to them: "Yes, the harvest is great, but the workers are few." There was much work to be done, so he added: "Beg the Master of the harvest to send out workers into his harvest." (Matt. 9:37, 38) Jesus instructed the disciples on how to go about their ministry. There was a sense of urgency in his words. He said: "You will by no means complete the circuit of the cities of Israel until the Son of man arrives."—Matt. 10:23.

Today, also, there is a great need in the field ministry. Time is running out, and this good news of the Kingdom must be preached before the end comes. (Mark 13:10) Since the field is the world, it is clear that we are faced with a situation quite similar to that experienced by Jesus and his disciples, only on a much larger scale. We too are few in number compared with the billions in the world of mankind, but we can be sure that Jehovah's hand is not short. He has the ability to have the Kingdom good news declared throughout the inhabited earth. The good news *will be preached* and the end *will come* on schedule according to Jehovah's own timetable. But will we then be found faithful as having discharged our responsibility to share in the ministry? (Ezek. 33: 8, 9) Will we put God's Kingdom first in our life now in order to accomplish our ministry fully? What theocratic goals are we pursuing to that end?

Expressing what Jehovah requires of each one of his dedicated servants, Jesus said: "You must love Jehovah your God with your whole heart and with your whole soul and with your whole mind and with your whole strength." (Mark 12:30) All of us are required to be whole-souled in our service to God. This means that we can individually demonstrate the depth of our devotion and the genuineness of our dedication by doing our utmost in the ministry. (2 Tim. 2:15) There are many opportunities open to each of us, according to our individual circumstances and abilities. Just consider what some of these opportunities are, and decide what theocratic goals you will pursue in fulfilling your ministry.

SERVING AS A CONGREGATION PUBLISHER

All who embrace the truth have the privilege of publishing the good news. This is the basic work that Jesus gave his disciples to do. (Matt. 24:14; 28:19, 20) A disciple of Jesus Christ usually begins speaking to others about the good news just as soon as he recognizes its value. This is what Andrew, Philip, Cornelius, and others did. (John 1:40, 41, 43-45; Acts 10:1, 2, 24; 16:14, 15, 25-34) Does this mean that a person may participate in telling others about the good news even before he gets baptized? Yes. As soon as an individual qualifies as an unbaptized publisher in the congregation, the opportunity to participate in the house-to-house preaching is open to him. Also, according to his ability and circumstances, he may regularly share in other features of the Christian ministry.

As a baptized member of the congregation, you are no doubt interested in doing all you can to help others learn the good news. Men and women alike have the privilege of sharing in the God-ordained preaching work. All should set a fine example in fulfilling their respective roles within the congregation. (1 Tim. 2:9-15; Titus 2:1-10; 1 Pet. 5:5) Male members of the congregation who make spiritual advancement and qualify may be appointed as ministerial servants. (1 Tim. 3:8-10, 12, 13) Such ones who reach out for the responsibilities of an overseer and who meet the Scriptural requirements are appointed to this office. They teach in the congregation and serve as shepherds of the flock. (1 Tim. 3:1-7; Titus 1:5-9) It is certainly a privilege to have even a small part in advancing the interests of God's Kingdom. Anyone who can expand his ministry to attain additional privileges of service is happy indeed.

SERVING WHERE THE NEED IS GREATER

It may be that you serve in a congregation where the territory is frequently worked and a fine witness is being given. If such is the case, you may feel that you could expand your ministry by moving to an area where there is a greater need in the field. (Acts 16:9) Your circuit overseer may have suggestions on how you can assist another congregation within the circuit. If you wish to serve in another area of your own country, you may write to the branch office for information. If you presently serve as an elder or a ministerial servant, there may be another congregation in your country that would appreciate having your assistance in caring for congregation needs.

Would you like to advance Kingdom interests in a foreign country? If so, you need to consider such a move carefully. It will certainly have an impact on you and any who accompany you. (Luke 14:28) If you are not planning to stay a long time, it may be best to consider serving in areas within your home country.

Before the branch office in your country or in another land can provide you with names of congregations that could benefit from your assistance, your Congregation Service Committee will need to provide a letter of recommendation. This letter is required whether you are serving as an elder, a ministerial servant, a pioneer, or a publisher. The service committee will send a letter of recommendation along with your inquiry directly to the branch office of the country where you desire to serve.

If serving where the need is greater is something that you would like to do, why not discuss the matter with the elders in your congregation? They may be able to help you determine how to go about making such a move or how to qualify for such service sometime in the future.

WORKING WITH A FOREIGN-LANGUAGE CONGREGATION

In order to expand your ministry, you may wish to consider learning another language, including a sign language. In some bilingual families, both parents and youths are serving in foreign-language congregations to care more fully for Kingdom interests. If you have the goal of learning to preach in another language, why not speak with the elders and the circuit overseer? They may be able to offer suggestions and needed encouragement. In some cases, under the direction of the branch office, circuits have organized language classes to help reach the local immigrant population.

AUXILIARY, REGULAR, AND SPECIAL PIONEER SERVICE

All publishers should be acquainted with the general requirements for auxiliary, regular, and special pioneer service as well as other branches of full-time service. From time to time, *Our Kingdom Ministry* sets out additional specific information. A pioneer publisher must be an exemplary baptized Christian whose personal circumstances allow him or her to spend the specified number of hours each month in publicly preaching the good news. The Congregation Service Committee approves applications for auxiliary pioneer service, whereas regular and special pioneers are appointed by the branch office.

Auxiliary pioneers may be appointed for a minimum of one month, for any number of consecutive months, or on a continuous basis, according to their circumstances. Many Kingdom publishers enjoy serving as auxiliary pioneers on special occasions, such as during the Memorial season or the month of the circuit overseer's visit. Some choose vacation months. Baptized, school-age publishers may wish to enroll as auxiliary pioneers during months they have time off from school. Whatever your personal circumstances, if you are maintaining a clean moral standing, can arrange to meet the specified hour requirement in the field ministry, and believe that you could serve one or more months as an auxiliary pioneer, the congregation elders will be pleased to consider your application for this privilege of service.

To qualify for appointment as a *regular pioneer,* you must currently be in a position to reach the yearly field service requirement. *Our Kingdom Ministry* suggests a monthly goal of hours that will assist you in fulfilling this responsibility. As a regular pioneer, you must always work in close cooperation with the congregation where you are serving. Zealous pioneers are a real blessing to a congregation, generating enthusiasm for the field ministry and even encouraging others to take up the pioneer service. Before the elders recommend that you be appointed as a regular pioneer, however, you must be baptized for at least six months, have good morals, and show yourself to be an exemplary publisher. You must be able to follow a practical schedule that will enable you to spend the required number of hours in field service.

Special pioneers are usually selected from among regular pioneers who have demonstrated their effectiveness in the ministry and who are able to serve wherever the branch office chooses to assign them. Often this is an isolated area where they can find interest and form new congregations. At times, special pioneers are assigned to congregations that need help in covering their territory regularly. Some special pioneers who are also elders have been assigned to help small congregations, even where there is not a particular need for more workers in the field. Special pioneers receive a modest reimbursement for necessary living expenses.

MINISTERIAL TRAINING SCHOOL

The steady increase in new congregations being formed each year gives evidence of Jehovah's blessing upon the efforts of his people to preach the good news of the Kingdom. (Acts 16:5) With the increase in congregations, the need for additional elders and ministerial servants also grows. Single brothers who qualify are encouraged to fill this need by saying to Jehovah: "Here I am! Send me." (Isa. 6:8) Many have responded in this way by applying to attend the Ministerial Training School, which is reserved for single ministerial servants and elders who are willing and able to serve where the need is greater. Such ones can learn more about the requirements by attending the meetings for brothers interested in the Ministerial Training School when these are held at circuit assemblies.

This school gives instruction in Bible teachings and in organizational matters so as to equip qualified men to handle congregational shepherding and other responsibilities. (Jer. 23:4) As a result of such training, some are assigned to serve where the need is greater in their own countries, whereas others receive assignments in foreign countries. Some are asked to return to their home congregations to help and encourage the local brothers and sisters. Those trained are better equipped to render spiritual and organizational help to God's people.—2 Tim. 3:16, 17.

MISSIONARY SERVICE

In order for the Kingdom good news to be preached "to the most distant part of the earth" before the end comes, it has been necessary to send missionaries forth into many lands. (Acts 1:8; Matt. 24:14) This has opened up opportunities for expanded service privileges for thousands of Jehovah's Witnesses, especially those who have already proved themselves to be zealous, whole-souled in their devotion, and effective in Kingdom service. Those invited to share in missionary work are usually given specialized training at the Watchtower Bible School of Gilead.

A person must have good physical health and stamina to qualify for missionary work, since many missionaries are assigned to countries where living conditions are difficult. Besides being exposed to diseases, a missionary may be required to adjust to a different standard of living and an entirely new culture.

If you are already in full-time service and would like to reach out for additional privileges as a missionary, you can learn more about the requirements by attending the meetings for those interested in missionary service when these are held at district conventions. Your circuit overseer may also be able to give you good advice. If you qualify, you may be privileged to take up this avenue of service that has contributed so much to the worldwide expansion of true worship.

BETHEL SERVICE

Serving at one of the many Bethel homes around the world is a special privilege. The name Bethel means "House of God," and that designation is certainly appropriate for these centers of theocratic activity. Brothers and sisters in Bethel service do a vital work in connection with producing and distributing literature used by Jehovah's Witnesses worldwide. From Brooklyn Bethel, the Governing Body provides oversight and direction for congregations throughout the earth.

Much of the service performed at Bethel is hard physical work. For this reason, those called into Bethel service are mainly dedicated, baptized brothers who are young in years, in good health, and physically strong. If there is a need in your country and you would like to serve at Bethel, you can learn more about the requirements by attending the special meetings for those interested in Bethel service when these are held at district conventions. Your circuit overseer can also be of assistance in this regard.

CONSTRUCTION VOLUNTEER

The construction of Kingdom Halls and Assembly Halls is a form of sacred service, similar to the work of constructing Solomon's temple. (1 Ki. 8:13-18) Many brothers and sisters show outstanding zeal for Jehovah's organization by volunteering their time and assets to support and have a part in this work.

Are you in a position to assist in this aspect of sacred service? If you are a baptized publisher and are willing to share in such activity, the Regional Building Committee would very much appreciate your offering to assist. If you are unskilled in building trades or are an unbaptized publisher in good standing in the congregation, you may be able to assist with the building of a Kingdom Hall in your area. Why not let the local elders and circuit overseer know of your availability to help? Some baptized publishers who qualify have even been in a position to volunteer for international construction work on Kingdom Hall and Assembly Hall projects in other countries.

WHAT ARE YOUR SPIRITUAL GOALS?

If you have dedicated your life to Jehovah, your expressed desire is to serve Jehovah forever. But what are your spiritual goals along the way? Having spiritual goals will help you to direct your energies and other resources wisely. (1 Cor. 9:26) You will be able to aim for something worthwhile. Such goals are conducive to spiritual growth and will help you to concentrate on the more important things as you reach out for additional service privileges.—Phil. 1:10; 1 Tim. 4:15, 16.

In his illustration of the sower, Jesus emphasized that good soil produces varying amounts of fruitage. He said: "As for the one sown upon the fine soil, this is the one hearing the word and getting the sense of it, who really does bear fruit and produces, this one a hundredfold, that one sixty, the other thirty." (Matt. 13:23) If we have got the sense of the word in our heart, should we not exert ourselves so as to produce abundant fruitage to Jehovah's praise? Do we not want to bear much Kingdom fruitage as we zealously share in the ministry? And do we not want to produce abundantly the fruitage of God's spirit in our life every day? (John 15:2, 3; Gal. 5:22, 23) Having spiritual goals can help us do all of that.

The apostle Paul set a fine example for us to imitate in our service to God. (1 Cor. 11:1) Paul exerted himself vigorously in serving Jehovah to the very best of his ability. He recognized that Jehovah's service provided him with many opportunities. To the brothers in Corinth, Paul wrote: "A large door that leads to activity has been opened to me." Is this not true in our case also? Are there not many opportunities for us to serve Jehovah in association with the congregation, especially in preaching the Kingdom good news? But like Paul, we must keep in mind that going through that "large door" involves contending with "many opposers." (1 Cor. 16:9) Paul was willing to discipline himself consistently, even as would an athlete whose heart's desire was to win a crown in the games, a crown that would quickly fade. Notice what Paul said: "I pummel my body and lead it as a slave." (1 Cor. 9:24-27) Are we of that same mind?

Many are serving as missionaries today because with encouragement from their parents and others, they set Gilead training and missionary work as a theocratic goal early in life, even while they were yet children. Similarly, many now serving at Bethel set Bethel service as a goal, either while they were very young or when they first became acquainted with the good news and learned about this special privilege of service.

According to differing personal circumstances in life, each one is encouraged to work toward theocratic goals. Some goals might be participating in field service each week, starting and conducting a home Bible study, making more time to prepare for congregation meetings, enrolling as an auxiliary or a regular pioneer, serving where the need is greater, constructing Kingdom Halls and Assembly Halls, serving at Bethel or in the missionary field. Of course, at congregation meetings, at conventions, and in the publications of Jehovah's Witnesses, attention may be drawn to other theocratic goals that you, according to your own personal circumstances, may want to consider and strive to reach. The important thing is that you remain steadfast and fully accomplish your ministry. If you do, you will honor God and reach your ultimate goal, that of serving Jehovah forever.—Luke 13:24; 1 Tim. 4:7b, 8.

CHAPTER 11

ARRANGEMENTS FOR PLACES OF WORSHIP

TRUE worshipers of Jehovah are commanded to assemble together to receive instruction and to encourage one another. (Deut. 31:12; Heb. 10:23-25) The first place of worship for God's chosen people —the Israelites—was "the tabernacle," or "the tent of meeting." (Ex. 39:32, 40) Later, David's son Solomon built a house, a temple, for God's glory. (1 Ki. 9:3) After that temple was destroyed in 607 B.C.E., the Jews arranged to meet in small buildings called synagogues to worship God. In time the temple was rebuilt, and once again, it served as a center of true worship. Jesus taught both in synagogues and in the temple. (Luke 4:16; John 18:20) Jesus even arranged for a meeting on a mountain to teach the crowds who were following him.—Matt. 5:1–7:29.

Eventually, separating themselves from those who turned aside from the truth, Jesus' disciples began to assemble in public places. (Acts 19:8, 9) Private homes were also used to teach the Scriptures and to enjoy association with true believers. (Rom. 16:3, 5; Col. 4:15; Philem. 2) Sometimes it was necessary for the early Christians to meet in isolated or secluded places to avoid detection by persecutors. Indeed, faithful servants of God in the past had a sincere desire to assemble in places of worship in order to be "taught by Jehovah."—Isa. 54:13.

Today, too, private homes and public places are used as Christian meeting places. Private homes often serve as locations of Congregation Book Studies or meetings for field service. Those who offer their home for such meetings, as circumstances require, view this as a privilege. Many report that they have benefited spiritually by opening their home in this way.

KINGDOM HALL

The principal meeting place of Jehovah's Witnesses is the Kingdom Hall. In some localities, it is more convenient to rent a hall than to buy or to build one. However, many congregations have chosen to purchase property and build their own Kingdom Hall suited to their needs. Or they have bought and renovated an existing building. In such cases, it is appropriate to have a dedication program. If only minor changes or renovations are made to an existing Kingdom Hall, there is no need to have a dedication program again.

The Kingdom Hall should not be an elaborate building made to impress others. While its design may vary from place to place, its purpose is functional. (Acts 17:24) In accord with local circumstances, it should be a comfortable and convenient place for holding Christian meetings.

Each Kingdom Hall is financed by the local congregation(s) of Jehovah's Witnesses. No collection plate is passed, nor is solicitation for funds made. A contribution box is provided, and those attending meetings have the privilege of caring for necessary expenses in connection with the use of the hall. They do so willingly, from the heart. (2 Cor. 9:7) Elders are generally familiar with information regarding ownership and operation of the Kingdom Hall as set out in *Our Kingdom Ministry,* memorandums, and letters provided by the branch office.

Those in the congregation should consider it a privilege to support the Kingdom Hall financially and to volunteer their services in keeping it clean, presentable, and in good repair. Both inside and out, the Kingdom Hall should properly represent Jehovah's organization. An elder or a ministerial servant is usually assigned to see that necessary work is cared for in accord with a list of things to be done each week. Generally, cleaning is arranged according to Congregation Book Study groups, with the book study overseer or his assistant taking the lead.

Where more than one congregation meets in a hall, the elders of the congregations involved will set up a Kingdom Hall Operating Committee to see that necessary maintenance is done on the building and property. The bodies of elders will designate a chairman. Working under the direction of the bodies of elders, the operating committee monitors the hall cleaning, making sure that the hall is kept in good repair and that sufficient supplies are on hand. Basically, the committee does the work that would be done by just one elder or ministerial servant if only one congregation met in the hall. Close cooperation among all involved is required.

When several congregations meet in one Kingdom Hall, any schedule of meeting times that involves rotation is worked out through the elders in a spirit of mutual concern and brotherly love. (Phil. 2:2-4; 1 Pet. 3:8) Whether the rotation is done once a year or once every few years is left up to the local congregations to decide. No one congregation should take it upon itself to make such decisions on behalf of other congregations. The rotation of meeting times should take place during the first week of the calendar year. When the circuit overseer visits one of the congregations in the Kingdom Hall, the other congregation(s) will adjust their meeting times as needed for that week.

The Kingdom Hall may be used for weddings and funerals with the permission of the Congregation Service Committee. These elders carefully consider what is requested and base their decision on direction provided by the branch office.

Those who are granted use of the Kingdom Hall for such purposes are expected to conduct themselves in a way that befits a place of true worship. All involved should be sure that nothing is done that would offend the congregation or bring reproach upon Jehovah and the good name of the congregation. (Phil. 2:14, 15) At times, use of the Kingdom Hall may be granted for other spiritual functions under the direction of the branch office, such as the Kingdom Ministry School and the Pioneer Service School.

The congregation should always treat their meeting places with respect. Dress, grooming, and decorum should bespeak the dignity associated with worshiping Jehovah. (Eccl. 5:1; 1 Tim. 2:9, 10) Applying counsel in this regard is a way of showing appreciation for our Christian meetings.

At meetings in the Kingdom Hall, qualified brothers are assigned to serve as attendants. They should be alert, have friendly personalities, and use good judgment. Their responsibilities include greeting newcomers and making them feel welcome, helping latecomers to find seats, recording attendance figures, and giving necessary attention to proper heating and ventilation of the hall. Maintaining order during the meetings is essential. It is recommended that children sit with their parents. When a child becomes unruly, an attendant might ask the parent in a kind and tactful way to take the child out, so that the audience will not be unduly distracted. Parents with young children can be encouraged to sit where they will cause the least distraction if it becomes necessary to take the children out to discipline them or to care for other needs.

Since the conduct of children inside the Kingdom Hall as well as outside can reflect favorably or unfavorably on the congregation, attendants should, where necessary, remind parents to give proper supervision, so that children do not run in the building or around the property before and after the meetings. The service performed by attendants obviously contributes much to everyone's enjoyment of the meetings. It is preferable that ministerial servants be used as attendants, particularly those who have had experience handling situations that arise in family life.—1 Tim. 3:12.

KINGDOM HALL CONSTRUCTION

At Kingdom Halls in many lands, there is a contribution box for the Kingdom Hall Fund. This fund is used to help finance the building of new Kingdom Halls and the renovation of those in need of repair.

Without such assistance, many congregations could not afford such an undertaking.

In the first century, certain Christians were more well-to-do than others, so the apostle Paul wrote: "By means of an equalizing your surplus just now might offset their deficiency, in order that their surplus might also come to offset your deficiency, that an equalizing might take place." (2 Cor. 8:14) Today a similar "equalizing" takes place, with some branches using a portion of the Kingdom Hall Fund to provide financial assistance to build Kingdom Halls for congregations in other lands where severe economic conditions prevail. The generous support of the worldwide brotherhood is greatly appreciated by the organization and by the congregations that directly benefit from these contributions.

In many lands, Regional Building Committees are appointed to oversee Kingdom Hall construction or renovation. Each committee is assigned to assist congregations in a particular region. Elders with secular experience in construction, real estate, business, accounting, and other related fields make up the committee, thus providing valuable guidance for a project from beginning to end.

If a Regional Building Committee is available in the area, elders should contact it before starting a Kingdom Hall project. The regional committee can assist a congregation in selecting suitable property and deciding on construction methods. It will also coordinate the use of workers who volunteer to help with construction. In support of this arrangement, all who qualify and desire to serve are encouraged to complete a volunteer worker application and give it to their local Congregation Service Committee for approval.

In cases of disaster, Regional Building Committees may be called upon to repair damaged Kingdom Halls and, on occasion, homes of the brothers. A Regional Building Committee may be assigned to assist with such work in other lands or to provide training for local brothers. At times, they may assist with construction of Assembly Halls and branch facilities. This entire arrangement is possible because God's people desire to do his will in a spirit of self-sacrifice. —Col. 3:23, 24.

Because of the great need for Kingdom Halls, especially in lands with limited resources, Kingdom Hall Construction Groups are organized. The brothers in these groups volunteer to move from one congregation to the next within a country to take the lead in support of building projects. This has sped up the construction work and has provided valuable training for local volunteers.

ASSEMBLY HALLS

Early Christians generally met in small groups. However, sometimes "quite a crowd" would assemble. (Acts 11:26) Similarly, Jehovah's people today meet in large gatherings for circuit assemblies and special assembly days. Local facilities are often rented for this purpose, but where such are not suitable or available, a place of worship called an Assembly Hall may be acquired.

At times, an existing building is purchased, renovated, and used as an Assembly Hall. More often, though, property is obtained, and a new hall is built. Assembly Halls vary in size, depending on local needs. The decision to construct such a building is made only after the branch office has carefully analyzed the cost and determined the amount of use it will have.

An Assembly Hall Committee is appointed by the branch office to oversee the operation of the Assembly Hall. Because of the size of these meeting places, full-time Assembly Hall personnel are appointed by the branch to care for the operation and maintenance involved. Arrangements are made for the circuits to clean the Assembly Hall. Special arrangements may be made for semiannual cleaning as well as for preventive maintenance. Rather than paying for services, it is beneficial for volunteers to do the work. Therefore, congregations are encouraged to support these arrangements wholeheartedly. —Ps. 110:3; Mal. 1:10.

At times, the Assembly Hall may also be used for other theocratic functions, such as the Ministerial Training School and special meetings for traveling overseers. Like the Kingdom Hall, an Assembly Hall is a dedicated place of worship. When we are meeting at an Assembly Hall, our conduct, dress, and grooming should bespeak the dignity associated with worshiping Jehovah.—Eccl. 5:1; 1 Tim. 2:9, 10.

The many new ones who are hastening to the organization during the final part of these last days are evidence of Jehovah's blessing. (Isa. 60:8, 10, 11, 22) Thus, we should wholeheartedly support the arrangements to obtain and maintain clean and comfortable places of worship, where we assemble to be instructed by Jehovah. In doing so, we show our appreciation for the role such facilities play in helping us to encourage one another all the more so as we behold Jehovah's day drawing near.

CHAPTER 12

SUPPORTING KINGDOM ACTIVITY LOCALLY AND WORLDWIDE

IN FULFILLMENT of Jesus' prophecy concerning the last days, Jehovah's Witnesses have carried the ministry of the good news "to the most distant part of the earth." (Acts 1:8; Matt. 24:14) In doing this, they have freely given of their time and energy in sharing spiritual things. Trusting in Jehovah to provide for his fellow workers, they have not become anxious but continue putting God's Kingdom first in their life. (Matt. 6:25-34; 1 Cor. 3:5-9) The results give clear evidence of Jehovah's approval and blessing.

CARING FOR KINGDOM INTERESTS WORLDWIDE

When viewing the methods used by Jehovah's Witnesses in preaching the good news today and realizing the extent of their distribution of Bible literature at no charge, some will ask: "How is all of this possible?" True, printing establishments that produce huge quantities of Bibles and Bible literature require money to operate. Much additional expense is incurred in the construction and maintenance of Bethel Homes for ministers who operate printing presses, oversee the preaching work, and in other ways serve full-time for the advancement of the good news. In addition, missionaries are trained and sent to many lands. Ministers are assigned as special pioneers, who spend their time working in isolated areas or with small congregations. Traveling overseers, who minister to congregations, are given some material assistance to help them continue in the work. Clearly, the work of supporting the ministry in our day, whether locally or worldwide, involves the outlay of large sums of money. Where does it all come from?

Although our literature is offered to the public without charge, many appreciate the work of Jehovah's Witnesses and are happy to donate to the worldwide work. Apart from this, the Witnesses themselves send voluntary contributions to local branch offices of Jehovah's Witnesses. Seeing the need, they demonstrate a willing spirit like that of God's ancient servants whose generous giving supported the building of Jehovah's place of worship. (Ex. 35:20-29; 1 Chron. 29:9) While some gifts are received from estates through wills, contributions from individuals, congregations, and circuits are usually sent in small amounts. When added together, these gifts provide enough to keep the ministry going.

So while sharing in the ministry of the good news, Jehovah's Witnesses also consider it a privilege to use their money and other material resources to advance the work. Jesus and his disciples maintained a money box from which funds were taken to help the poor and to care for expenses. (John 12:6; 13:28, 29) The Bible tells us of women who gave material support to the ministry of Jesus and his disciples. (Mark 15:40, 41; Luke 8:3) The apostle Paul gratefully accepted loving material assistance from those who were interested in advancing the good news and who wished to have a share in his ministry. (Phil. 4:14-16; 1 Thess. 2:9) Jehovah's Witnesses continue to follow these ancient patterns of zealous service and generous giving. Thus, it is possible for honesthearted ones everywhere to be offered 'the waters of life free.'—Rev. 22:17.

CARING FOR THE NEEDS OF THE LOCAL CONGREGATION

The expenses of the local congregation are also covered by voluntary contributions. No collections are taken, nor is there an assessment of dues or a solicitation of money; but contribution boxes are provided at meeting places so that each person can have a part in giving "just as he has resolved in his heart."—2 Cor. 9:7.

Money contributed is principally used to pay for the operation and upkeep of the Kingdom Hall. The body of elders might decide that some of the money could be sent to the local branch office of Jehovah's Witnesses for use in furthering the worldwide Kingdom activity. If so, a resolution to this effect would be adopted by the congregation. In this way, many congregations make regular contributions to the worldwide work. Other needs may arise from time to time, but when all are alert to local needs, it should not be necessary to make frequent announcements regarding contributions.

HANDLING CONTRIBUTIONS

After each meeting, two elders or ministerial servants who have been assigned by the body of elders remove any money that may have been deposited in the contribution boxes and make a record of it. (2 Cor. 8:20) The body of elders will make appropriate arrangements for safeguarding these funds until they can be forwarded to the branch office or used for congregation needs. This may require the opening of a congregation bank account. The brother handling the congregation accounts prepares a monthly statement to inform the congregation, and every three months the presiding overseer arranges for an audit of the accounts. A reminder of this is published regularly in *Our Kingdom Ministry*.

FINANCING CIRCUIT ASSEMBLIES AND SPECIAL ASSEMBLY DAYS

Expenses incurred in operating assemblies are defrayed by contributions from the Witnesses making up the circuit. Contribution boxes are provided at the assemblies, just as they are at congregation meetings. In this way, voluntary contributions can be made to the circuit. A brother selected by the circuit overseer handles the circuit accounts, paying bills that are approved by the circuit overseer.

Ideally, each assembly is to pay the expenses it incurs, with surplus funds being deposited in the circuit account. If a deficit should occur at the end of an assembly and circuit funds can cover the loss, there is no need to write the congregations regarding the difference. However, if there are insufficient funds in the circuit account to pay expenses for the last assembly or to meet initial expenses for the next assembly, such as a deposit to secure the use of a facility, the circuit overseer may direct that congregations be advised of the privilege to contribute. Each body of elders will discuss the matter and determine what contribution their congregation would be able to make to the circuit fund. They would then handle this in their congregation by means of a resolution.

When meeting together in connection with an assembly, the circuit elders decide what should be done with the funds that the circuit has at its disposal. Decisions need to be made regarding the assembly operating expenses, purchase of circuit equipment, and expenses incurred by the traveling overseers while serving the circuit. Consideration may be given to making donations to the worldwide work, the Kingdom Hall Fund, a local Assembly Hall, or some other important need.

All decisions other than those involving recurring operating expenses should be put in writing as resolutions adopted by the elders. These resolutions must be for exact amounts and presented for approval each time circuit funds are dispensed. It is inappropriate to pass standing resolutions or those not for specific amounts. Money belonging to the circuit may be deposited with the branch office for safekeeping until such time as the circuit needs it.

The circuit overseer will arrange for an audit of the circuit accounts following each circuit assembly and special assembly day.

CARING FOR THE POOR

One purpose of the money box maintained by Jesus and his disciples was to help the poor. (Mark 14:3-5; John 13:29) That Christian responsibility has continued, for Jesus said: "You always have the poor with you." (Mark 14:7) How do Jehovah's Witnesses discharge their responsibility in this regard today?

At times, faithful ones in the congregation may be in need of material assistance because of advanced age, infirmity, or some adversity beyond their control. Individuals in the congregation who become aware of such a need may feel moved to act in harmony with the words of the apostle John: "Whoever has this world's means for supporting life and beholds his brother having need and yet shuts the door of his tender compassions upon him, in what way does the love of God remain in him? Little children, let us love, neither in word nor with the tongue, but in deed and truth." (1 John 3:17, 18; 2 Thess. 3:6-12)

True worship includes looking after faithful and loyal ones who may be in need of material assistance. —Jas. 1:27; 2:14-17.

In his first letter to Timothy, the apostle Paul explained how material assistance may be provided to deserving ones. You can read his counsel at 1 Timothy 5:3-21. The primary responsibility rests with each Christian to care for the needs of his own household. Older or infirm ones should receive assistance from their children, grandchildren, or other close relatives. At times, material assistance is available through governmental or social agencies, so relatives or others may show kindness in helping the needy one to make proper requests for such assistance. A situation may arise where it might become necessary for the congregation as a whole to consider providing some form of assistance to certain needy brothers and sisters who have a long history of faithful service. If there are no family members or other relatives to assist such ones and no adequate assistance from governmental or social agencies is available, the body of elders can make appropriate recommendations to provide some help. Faithful Christians consider it a privilege to share their material possessions with these ones in times of need.

Many of our brothers may come to be in need because of persecution, wars, earthquakes, floods, famines, or other calamitous occurrences that are common in these critical times. (Matt. 24:7-9) On such occasions, local congregations may not have anything to share with one another, so the Governing Body coordinates the efforts of brothers elsewhere to provide what is needed. This is similar to the way Christians in Asia Minor provided food for the brothers in Judea during a time of famine. (1 Cor. 16:1-4; 2 Cor. 9:1-5) By following their example, we confirm our love for our brothers and show ourselves to be genuine disciples of Jesus Christ. —John 13:35.

LITERATURE DISTRIBUTION

The distribution of Bibles and Bible literature plays an important role in spreading the Kingdom message. Usually a ministerial servant is assigned by the body of elders to look after the congregation's supply of books, booklets, brochures, and so forth, and another is assigned to care for the magazines. All such literature is made available to the publishers, who, in turn, offer it to those who show interest.

The brothers assigned to look after these supplies take their responsibilities seriously. They keep a written record of all movement of stock. By keeping informed as to what literature is available and by monitoring the flow of literature to the field, they can arrange to have an adequate supply on hand to care for the needs of the congregation. Since Bible literature has proved to be so effective in spreading the good news, publishers are encouraged to feature it in their ministry. *Our Kingdom Ministry* announces a specific literature offer for each month so as to ensure an orderly and thorough witness throughout the territory.

As dedicated Christians, we recognize that our time, mental and physical assets, talents, material possessions, even our very life are gifts from God and intended for use in his service. (Luke 17:10; 1 Cor. 4:7) By making proper use of all our resources, we demonstrate the depth of our love and devotion to Jehovah. It is our desire to honor

Jehovah with our valuable things, knowing that he is pleased with any gift that is given as an expression of whole-souled devotion. (Prov. 3:9; Mark 14:3-9; Luke 21:1-4; Col. 3:23, 24) By maintaining a proper view of material things and a generous spirit, we experience the fulfillment of Jesus' words: "You received free, give free." We, in turn, receive the greater joy.—Matt. 10:8b; Acts 20:35.

CHAPTER 13

"DO ALL THINGS FOR GOD'S GLORY"

AS God's dedicated servants bearing his name, we are under obligation to reflect Jehovah's glory in all that we say and do. The apostle Paul offered a guiding principle when he wrote: "Whether you are eating or drinking or doing anything else, do all things for God's glory." (1 Cor. 10:31) This involves our holding to Jehovah's righteous standards, which are a reflection of his own perfect personality. (Col. 3:10) We must become imitators of God, as a holy people.—Eph. 5:1, 2.

Calling this need to the attention of Christians, the apostle Peter wrote: "As obedient children, quit being fashioned according to the desires you formerly had in your ignorance, but, in accord with the Holy One who called you, do you also become holy yourselves in all your conduct, because it is written: 'You must be holy, because I am holy.'" (1 Pet. 1:14-16) Like Israel of old, members of the Christian congregation are required to maintain holiness. This means that they are to remain untarnished, clean from sinful contamination and worldliness. They are thus set apart for Jehovah's service.—Ex. 20:5.

Holiness is maintained by adhering to Jehovah's laws and principles. These are clearly set out in the Holy Scriptures. (2 Tim. 3:16) Through a study of the Scriptures, we were taught about Jehovah and his ways, and we were drawn to him. Becoming one of his people was not just a matter of accepting a few basic doctrines and then getting baptized in water. Our study of the Bible convinced us of the need to seek first God's Kingdom and to make the doing of Jehovah's will paramount in our life. (Matt. 6:33; Rom. 12:2) In effect, this required that we put on the new personality.—Eph. 4:22-24.

SPIRITUAL AND MORAL CLEANNESS

Living up to our dedication by holding to Jehovah's righteous standards is not always easy. Our Adversary, Satan the Devil, seeks to turn us aside from the truth. Wicked influences from the world around us and the sinful tendencies of our fallen flesh make things difficult at times. All of this requires a spiritual fight on our part. The Scriptures tell us not to be puzzled when we encounter opposition or trials. We will have to suffer for the sake of righteousness. (2 Tim. 3:12) We can be happy while undergoing trials, knowing that such trials are proof that we are doing God's will.—1 Pet. 3:14-16; 4:14-16.

Though Jesus was perfect, he learned obedience by the things he suffered. At no time did he yield to Satan's temptations or develop worldly aspirations. (Matt. 4:1-11; John 6:15) Not once did Jesus even give thought to compromise. Although his faithful course incurred the world's hatred, he always held to Jehovah's righteous standards. Shortly before his death, Jesus warned his disciples that just as the world had hated him because he was no part of it, so the world would hate them. From that time forward, followers of Jesus Christ have experienced tribulation, but they have taken courage in knowing that the Son of God conquered the world.—John 15:19; 16:33; 17:16.

For us to overcome the world, we need to uphold Jehovah's righteous standards, as our Master did. In addition to avoiding involvement with the world in its political and social fields, we must resist the world's degraded moral climate. So we should take seriously the counsel found at James 1:21: "Put away all filthiness and that superfluous thing, badness, and accept with mildness the implanting of the word which is able to save your souls." By regularly implanting the word of truth in our mind and heart through study and meeting attendance, we keep strong in faith, even in the face of temptations and trials. Although worldly elements exert a strong influence, we must not even begin to desire what the world offers. Why not? Pointedly, the disciple James warns: "Do you not know that the friendship with the world is enmity with God? Whoever, therefore, wants to be a friend of the world is constituting himself an enemy of God." (Jas. 4:4) Can you see why the Bible contains strong admonition that we hold to Jehovah's righteous standards and remain separate from the world?

The inspired counsel of God's Word warns us against sharing in shameful and immoral conduct. It tells us that 'fornication and uncleanness of every sort or greediness should not even be mentioned among us, just as it befits holy people.' So we must refuse to allow our mind to dwell upon things that are obscene, shameful, or base, and we should not discuss such things in unnecessary conversation. We must avoid watching immoral and unclean entertainment. (Eph. 5:3-5) Thereby we give proof of wanting to hold to Jehovah's clean and righteous standards of morality.

PHYSICAL CLEANLINESS

Along with spiritual and moral cleanness, Christians recognize the importance of being physically clean. In ancient Israel, the God of holiness required that the camp be kept clean. (Deut. 23:14) The way of life then had to conform to Jehovah's standards of cleanliness. Our way of life too must be kept clean so that Jehovah 'may see nothing indecent in us.'

Holiness and physical cleanliness are closely linked in the Bible. For example, Paul wrote: "Beloved ones, let us cleanse ourselves of every defilement of flesh and spirit, perfecting holiness in God's fear." (2 Cor. 7:1) True Christians, therefore, should strive to keep their bodies clean by regularly washing their clothes and by bathing. While conditions vary from country to country, Christian men and women can generally find enough soap and water to keep their bodies clean and to see that their children are kept clean.

In view of our public witnessing, we are usually well-known in the community where we live. Keeping a neat and orderly home, inside and out, is in itself a witness to the neighbors. This is something in which the whole family can be involved. Husbands and fathers should take particular interest in the home and its surroundings, knowing that a tidy yard and well-kept home merit favorable testimony from those on the outside. Family heads recognize that this, along with their taking the lead in spiritual matters, is an indication that they are presiding well over their own household. (1 Tim. 3:4, 12) Wives and mothers have a responsibility to care for things too, especially inside the home. (Titus 2:4, 5) Well-trained children do their part in keeping themselves as well as their rooms neat and clean. Thus the entire family works together in developing habits and patterns of cleanliness that will fit in with the new world under God's Kingdom.

Many of Jehovah's servants today use automobiles for transportation to meetings and in field service. In some areas a car has become virtually indispensable in the ministry. As such, it should be kept clean and in good repair. Our homes and automobiles should testify that we are part of Jehovah's clean and holy people.

Our dress and grooming should be in keeping with godly principles. We would not think of appearing before prominent human officials if we were dressed in a slovenly or careless manner. How much more concerned we should be when serving Jehovah, representing him in the field ministry or on the platform! Our grooming and clothing styles can influence how others view the worship of Jehovah. It certainly would not be fitting to be immodest or inconsiderate of others. (Mic. 6:8; 1 Cor. 10:31-33; 1 Tim. 2:9, 10) Hence, when we are getting ready to participate in the field ministry or to assemble for worship at congregation meetings, circuit assemblies, and larger conventions, we should have in mind what the Scriptures say about physical cleanliness and modest appearance, so as to honor and glorify Jehovah always.

The same would apply when visiting any of the branch offices of Jehovah's Witnesses. Remember, the name Bethel means "House of God." Therefore, our dress, grooming, and conduct should be similar to what is expected of us when attending meetings for worship at the Kingdom Hall.

WHOLESOME RECREATION AND ENTERTAINMENT

The need for some rest and refreshment is recognized. Once Jesus invited his disciples to come with him to a lonely place and "rest up a bit." (Mark 6:31) A period of rest as well as wholesome recreation or entertainment can provide some pleasant diversion. It can refresh us so that we can press ahead with our normal work.

With so many forms of recreation available, Christians need to be selective and exercise godly wisdom in what they do. While recreation has its place, it is not the big thing in life. We are warned that in "the last days," men would become "lovers of pleasures rather than lovers of God." (2 Tim. 3:1, 4) Much of what is today termed "recreation" and "entertainment" is objectionable to those who desire to hold to Jehovah's righteous standards.

The early Christians had to resist the unwholesome environment in the pleasure-seeking world around them. At the Roman circus, spectators were entertained by viewing the sufferings of others. Violence, bloodshed, and sexual immorality were key elements in the recreation of the populace, but the early Christians stayed away from such things. Much of the modern world's entertainment features similar elements and caters to base human appetites. We need to 'keep strict watch on how we walk,' turning away from demoralizing entertainment. (Eph. 5:15, 16; Ps. 11:5) And even though the entertainment itself may be acceptable, often the presence and influence of worldly people are harmful.—1 Pet. 4:1-4.

There are wholesome forms of recreation and entertainment that Christians can engage in to enjoy a change of pace and refresh their physical and mental powers. Many have benefited from following the Scriptural counsel and balanced suggestions that can be found in the publications of Jehovah's Witnesses.

At times, several families may be invited to a home for Christian fellowship. Or brothers and sisters may be invited to attend a wedding reception or a similar social occasion. (John 2:2) Reasonably, those who are hosts in such cases should feel personally responsible for what takes place. With this in mind, discerning Christians have seen the wisdom of limiting the size and duration of such gatherings. If alcoholic beverages are served at all, they should be used in moderation. (Phil. 4:5) If every effort is made to ensure that Christian get-togethers are wholesome and spiritually refreshing, food and drink will not be the most important consideration.

Clearly, there is need for caution when large groups get together. The relaxed atmosphere at such gatherings has led some to go beyond the limits of proper Christian conduct, becoming involved in excessive eating and drinking and even other serious wrongdoing.

It is a fine thing to be hospitable. (1 Pet. 4:9) When inviting others to our home for a meal, refreshments, relaxation, and fellowship, we want to keep in mind those in the congregation who may be disadvantaged. (Luke 14:12-14) If we are guests on such occasions, our conduct should be in line with the counsel found at Mark 12:31. It is always good to show appreciation for the kindness of others.

Christians rejoice in God's bounteous gifts and find that they can 'eat and indeed drink and see good for all their hard work.' (Eccl. 3:12, 13) By ensuring that these and other activities are always done to God's glory, hosts as well as guests will look back on social gatherings, not with a troubled conscience, but with the satisfaction of having been spiritually refreshed.

SCHOOL ACTIVITIES

Children of Jehovah's Witnesses benefit from getting a basic secular education. While attending school, they are interested in learning how to read and write well. Other subjects taught in primary school as well as in high school can be of value to young people as they pursue spiritual goals. During their school years, they want to make a diligent effort to 'remember their Creator' by putting spiritual things first.—Eccl. 12:1.

If you are a Christian youth attending school, you need to exercise special care. When worldly youths go unrestrained in their rebellious conduct, you must not side with them. (2 Tim. 3:1, 2) Under these circumstances, there is much you can do to ward off worldly influences. Jehovah has not left any of us exposed to dangers without providing the necessary protection. (Ps. 23:4; 91:1, 2) So take advantage of Jehovah's provisions; this will serve to safeguard you.—Ps. 23:5.

To keep separate from the world while in school, young Witnesses should consider the danger of becoming involved in extracurricular activities. Classmates and teachers may not always understand your decision not to participate. However, pleasing God is what counts. This requires that you exercise your Bible-trained conscience and stand firm in the resolve not to become involved in worldly competition or nationalistic practices, which violate Bible principles. (Gal. 5:19, 26) By listening to the Scriptural counsel of godly parents and benefiting from the good association and instruction of the congregation, you young ones will be aided in holding to Jehovah's righteous standards.

SECULAR WORK AND ASSOCIATES

Family heads have a Scriptural obligation to provide for the needs of their own household. (1 Tim. 5:8) Even so, as ministers they recognize that their secular work is secondary to the pursuit of vital Kingdom interests. (Matt. 6:33; Rom. 11:13) By practicing godly devotion and being content with sustenance and covering, they avoid the anxieties and snares of the materialistic way of life so common in the world.—1 Tim. 6:6-10.

Not only family heads but all dedicated Christians who find it necessary to be secularly employed should have Scriptural principles in mind. Making honest provision for ourselves means that we refuse to engage in activities that violate God's law or that are against the law of the land. (Rom. 13: 1, 2; 1 Cor. 6:9, 10) Also, there is a need to be constantly aware of the dangers of bad association. As soldiers of Christ, we refrain from engaging in commercial endeavors that violate Christian standards or jeopardize our spirituality. (2 Tim. 2:4) Neither do we have connections with God's religious enemy, "Babylon the Great."—Rev. 18:2, 4; 2 Cor. 6:14-17.

Observing God's righteous standards will prevent us from taking advantage of our theocratic association in order to promote personal or other business interests. The purpose of our association with others at Christian meetings in the local congregation and when attending circuit assemblies and conventions is exclusively to worship Jehovah, feeding at his spiritual table and enjoying an interchange of encouragement. (Rom. 1:11, 12; Heb. 10:24, 25) Such association should be kept on a spiritual level.

DWELLING IN CHRISTIAN UNITY

Jehovah's righteous standards for his people also require that they "observe the oneness of the spirit in the uniting bond of peace." (Eph. 4:1-3) Rather than seeking to please himself, each one seeks to pursue what is good toward others. This is no doubt the spirit you have found in your association with the Christian congregation. No matter what our racial, national, social, economic, or educational background may be, all of us are governed by the same righteous standards. Even outsiders have observed this outstanding characteristic of Jehovah's people.—1 Pet. 2:12.

Further emphasizing the basis for unity, the apostle Paul writes: "One body there is, and one spirit, even as you were called in the one hope to which you were called; one Lord, one faith, one baptism; one God and Father of all persons, who is over all and through all and in all." (Eph. 4:4-6) How forcefully this calls for unity in understanding basic Bible doctrine as well as more advanced Bible teaching in recognition of Jehovah's sovereign will and authority! Truly, Jehovah has given his people the pure language of truth, which enables them to serve shoulder to shoulder. —Zeph. 3:9.

The unity and peace of the Christian congregation today is certainly a source of refreshment for all who worship Jehovah. We have experienced the fulfillment of Jehovah's promise: "In unity I shall set them, like a flock in the pen." (Mic. 2:12) We want to maintain that peaceful unity by living daily as a holy people, always holding to Jehovah's righteous standards.

Happy are those who have been accepted into the clean congregation of Jehovah! To be called by Jehovah's name is worth every sacrifice we may have to make. As we maintain our precious relationship with Jehovah, we will strive diligently to hold to his righteous standards and to recommend them to others. —2 Cor. 3:18.

CHAPTER 14

MAINTAINING THE PEACE AND CLEANNESS OF THE CONGREGATION

EACH year thousands of people flock to Jehovah's house of pure worship, in fulfillment of Bible prophecy. (Mic. 4:1, 2) How happy we are to receive them into "the congregation of God"! (Acts 20:28) They appreciate the opportunity to serve Jehovah with us and to enjoy our spiritual paradise. This spiritually clean and peaceful environment is made possible by the operation of Jehovah's holy spirit and by our applying the wise counsel found in his Word, the Bible.—Ps. 119:105; Zech. 4:6.

Application of Bible principles enables us to put on the Christian personality. (Col. 3:10) We make every effort to conform our way of life to Jehovah's righteous standards. For this reason, we put aside petty disputes and personal differences. By accepting Jehovah's view of matters, we overcome divisive worldly influences, and this allows us to work unitedly in love as an international brotherhood.—Acts 10:34, 35.

Nevertheless, from time to time difficulties arise, affecting the peace and unity of the congregation. What is the cause? In most cases, it is a failure to heed and apply Bible counsel. We still have to cope with our imperfect human tendencies. Not one of us is without sin. (1 John 1:10) Someone may, without fully realizing it, take a false step that could introduce moral or spiritual uncleanness into the congregation. By our thoughtless action or unguarded tongue, we may offend someone, or we may feel offended because of what someone has said or done. (Rom. 3:23) When such difficulties arise, what can we do to set matters straight?

We can be thankful that Jehovah has lovingly taken all of this into consideration. His Word provides counsel on what to do when difficulties arise on account of inherited imperfections and limitations or when wrongdoing is introduced into the congregation. Personal assistance is available from loving spiritual shepherds. By applying their Scriptural counsel, we can enjoy a fine relationship with all in the congregation and maintain a good standing with Jehovah. If we require discipline or reproof because of some wrongdoing on our part, we can be sure that such correction is an expression of our heavenly Father's love for us.—Prov. 3:11, 12; Heb. 12:6.

SETTLING MINOR DIFFERENCES

There may be times when personal disputes or difficulties of a minor nature arise between individual members of the congregation. These should quickly be settled in a spirit of brotherly love. (Eph. 4:26; Phil. 2:2-4; Col. 3:12-14) Very likely you will find that most problems of a personal nature involving your relationship with another member of the congregation can be resolved by applying the apostle Peter's counsel to "have intense love for one another, because love covers a multitude of sins." (1 Pet. 4:8) Such minor difficulties stem from human imperfection. We all stumble many times. (Jas. 3:2) By recognizing this and applying the Golden Rule, doing to others just as we would want them to do to us, we can usually dispose of minor offenses by forgiving and forgetting.—Matt. 7:12.

But if something has disturbed your relationship with someone in the congregation so much that you feel that another approach is needed, wisdom dictates that you do not delay in resolving the matter, knowing that your relationship with Jehovah is also involved. Jesus counseled his disciples: "If, then, you are bringing your gift to the altar and you there remember that your brother has something against you, leave your gift there in front of the altar, and go away; first make your peace with your brother, and then, when you have come back, offer up your gift." (Matt. 5:23, 24) There may have been a misunderstanding. If so, it should be cleared up by giving priority to Christian unity and keeping the lines of communication open. Good communication among all in the congregation goes a long way toward preventing misunderstandings and resolving problems that arise because of human imperfection.

PROVIDING NEEDED SCRIPTURAL COUNSEL

At times, overseers may find it necessary to counsel someone, trying to readjust his thinking. This is not always easy. To the Christians in Galatia, the apostle Paul wrote: "Brothers, even though a man takes some false step before he is aware of it, you who have spiritual qualifications try to readjust such a man in a spirit of mildness."—Gal. 6:1.

By lovingly caring for the flock, overseers protect the congregation from many spiritual dangers and prevent serious problems from developing. Shepherds of the flock should strive to make their service to the congregation measure up to Jehovah's promise through Isaiah: "Each one must prove to be like a hiding place from the wind and a place of concealment from the rainstorm, like streams of water in a waterless country, like the shadow of a heavy crag in an exhausted land."—Isa. 32:2.

RESOLVING CERTAIN SERIOUS WRONGS

Willingness to overlook offenses and to forgive does not mean that we are unconcerned about wrongdoing or that we approve of it. Not all wrongs can be charged to inherited imperfection; nor is it for our brother's good or for the good of the congregation to overlook wrongs that go beyond minor offenses. (Lev. 19:17; Ps. 141:5) The Law covenant recognized degrees of seriousness of sins and transgressions. This is also true in the Christian arrangement.—1 John 5:16, 17.

Jesus outlined some specific procedures for resolving problems involving serious wrongdoing that may arise between fellow Christians. Note the steps that he set out: "If your brother commits a sin, [1] go lay bare his fault between you and him alone. If he listens to you, you have gained your brother. But if he does not listen, [2] take along with you one or two more, in order that at the mouth of two or three witnesses every matter may be established. If he does not listen to them, [3] speak to the congregation. If he does not listen even to the congregation, let him be to you just as a man of the nations and as a tax collector."—Matt. 18:15-17.

The illustration that Jesus subsequently gave, recorded at Matthew 18:23-35, shows that the sins considered at Matthew 18:15-17 are evidently such sins as those involving financial or property matters —failure to make proper payment for something or some action involving a measure of fraud—or the damaging of someone's reputation by actual slander.

If you have solid evidence that someone in the congregation has committed such a serious sin against you personally, do not be hasty to turn to the overseers or others, asking them to intervene on your behalf. As Jesus counseled, speak first with the one against whom you have a complaint. Try to resolve the matter between just the two of you without involving anyone else. If he does not respond favorably to your efforts, you may let a little time pass before taking the matter further. Keep in mind that Jesus did not say *'go only once,* and lay bare his fault.' Therefore, if the person does not initially admit the wrong and ask forgiveness, it may be good to consider approaching him again later. If the matter can be straightened out in this way, the one who sinned will certainly appreciate that you have not told others about his sin or marred his good reputation in the congregation. You will have achieved your objective of 'gaining your brother.'

If the one who committed the offense accepts responsibility, seeks forgiveness, and straightens the matter out, there is no need to carry the matter further. This shows that although serious, the offenses here discussed are limited to those that can be settled between the individuals involved. This does not include such offenses as fornication, adultery, homosexuality, blasphemy, apostasy, idolatry, and similar gross sins. (1 Cor. 6:9, 10; Gal. 5:19-21) These sins require more than forgiveness from an offended individual. Since the spiritual and moral cleanness of the congregation may be threatened, such matters should be reported to the elders and handled by them.—1 Cor. 5:6; Jas. 5:14, 15.

If you are not able to gain your brother by 'laying bare his fault between you and him alone,' then you may do as Jesus said—take along one or two others and speak with your brother again. Those you take with you should also have the objective of gaining your brother. Preferably, they would be witnesses of the alleged wrongdoing, but if there are no eyewitnesses, you may choose to take along brothers to be witnesses to the discussion. They may have experience in the matter at issue and may be able to establish whether what occurred was truly a wrong. Elders chosen as witnesses do not represent the congregation, since the body of elders has not specifically assigned them in the matter.

If you are convinced that your brother has committed a serious sin against you and you have evidence to prove it and the matter has not been resolved after repeated efforts—when you spoke with him alone and when you went to him with one or two others—and you feel that you cannot let it pass, then you should report the matter to the overseers of the congregation. Remember that their goal too is to maintain the peace and cleanness of the congregation. Having approached the elders, you will have taken the matter as far as you can. Leave the problem in their hands, and trust in Jehovah that it will be resolved. Never should you allow the conduct of someone else to stumble you or to rob you of your joy in Jehovah's service.—Ps. 119:165.

If upon investigation it becomes evident to the shepherds of the flock that the brother has indeed committed a serious sin against you and yet has been unwilling to repent and try to make reasonable and appropriate amends, it may become necessary for the overseers to expel the unrepentant wrongdoer.

In that way they protect the flock and safeguard the cleanness of the congregation.—Matt. 18:17.

MARKING DISORDERLY ONES

In his second letter to the Thessalonians, Paul warned of certain ones who were walking disorderly and who if accorded good standing in the congregation could exert an unhealthy influence. Paul admonished the Thessalonian Christians "to withdraw from every brother walking disorderly and not according to the tradition you received from us." He further clarified that statement by writing: "If anyone is not obedient to our word through this letter, keep this one marked, stop associating with him, that he may become ashamed. And yet do not be considering him as an enemy, but continue admonishing him as a brother."—2 Thess. 3:6, 14, 15.

Occasionally, someone not known to be guilty of practicing a grave sin for which he could be expelled nevertheless displays flagrant disregard for theocratic order. This could include such things as being grossly lazy or critical, being a profitless talker who is a constant 'meddler with what does not concern him.' (2 Thess. 3:11) Or this could include one who is scheming to take material advantage of others or indulging in entertainment that is clearly improper. The disorderly conduct is not so minor that it can be handled by applying Bible counsel and manifesting love; rather, it is serious enough to reflect badly on the congregation and potentially to spread to other Christians.

After giving repeated admonition to such an individual and finding that he persists in disregarding well-established Bible principles, the elders may decide that a talk should be given to the congregation providing appropriate counsel concerning such disorderly conduct. Elders will use reasonableness and discernment in determining whether a particular situation is sufficiently serious and disturbing to require a warning talk. This talk will not name the disorderly one. However, those who are aware of the situation described in the talk will take heed and limit their social contacts with such individuals.

The loving concern and firm stand of faithful members of the congregation could indeed move the disorderly one to shame and repentance. When it is clearly evident that the individual has abandoned his disorderly course, it would no longer be necessary to treat him as a marked individual.

HANDLING CASES OF SERIOUS WRONGDOING

After taking the steps outlined at Matthew 18:15, 16, some individual brothers or sisters may report to the elders cases of unresolved serious wrongdoing. (Matt. 18:17) On the other hand, individuals may also approach the elders either to confess their own sin or to report what they know regarding the wrongdoing of others. (Lev. 5:1; Jas. 5:16) Regardless of the manner in which the elders first hear reports of serious wrongdoing on the part of a baptized member of the congregation, an initial investigation will be made by two elders. If it is established that there is substance to the report and that evidence is available showing that a serious sin actually has been committed, the body of elders will assign a judicial committee of at least three elders to handle the matter. Regarding serious wrongdoing by one who is unbaptized, see pages 157-8.

While exercising watchful care of the flock, seeking to protect it from any elements that would be spiritually damaging, the elders will also endeavor to use God's Word skillfully to reprove any who have erred and will try to restore them. (Jude 21-23) This is in harmony with instructions given to Timothy by the apostle Paul, who wrote: "I solemnly charge you before God and Christ Jesus, who is destined to judge the living and the dead, . . . reprove, reprimand, exhort, with all long-suffering and art of teaching." (2 Tim. 4:1, 2) Doing so may take much time and effort, but this is part of the hard work of the elders. The congregation appreciates their endeavors and gives them double honor.—1 Tim. 5:17.

In every situation where guilt is established, the primary endeavor of the overseers is to restore the wrongdoer if he is genuinely repentant as indicated, for example, by his producing "works that befit repentance." (Acts 26:20) If he is repentant and they are able to help him, their administering reproof either in private or before onlookers with knowledge of the case serves to discipline him and instill a wholesome fear in any such onlookers. (2 Sam. 12:13; 1 Tim. 5:20) In all cases of judicial reproof, restrictions are imposed. Thus the wrongdoer may be helped to 'make straight paths for his feet' thereafter. (Heb. 12:13) In due course these restrictions are removed as the individual's spiritual recovery becomes manifest.

ANNOUNCEMENT OF REPROOF

If a judicial committee determines that an individual is repentant but that the matter is likely to become known in the congregation or in the community or if for other reasons the elders believe that the congregation needs to be advised, a simple announcement will be made during the Service Meeting. It should read: "[Name of person] has been reproved." The presiding overseer should approve this announcement.

IF THE DECISION IS TO DISFELLOWSHIP

In some cases the wrongdoer may become hardened in his course of sinful conduct and thus fail to respond to efforts to help him. Fruitage, or works, befitting repentance may not be in evidence, nor may genuine repentance be apparent at the time of the judicial hearing. What then? In such cases, it is necessary to expel the unrepentant wrongdoer from the congregation, thus denying him fellowship with Jehovah's clean congregation. This is done to remove the bad influence of the wrongdoer from the congregation, thereby safeguarding the moral and spiritual cleanness of the congregation and protecting its good name. (Deut. 21:20, 21; 22:23, 24) When the apostle Paul became aware of the shameful conduct of a member of the congregation in Corinth, he admonished the elders to "hand such a man over to Satan . . . in order that the spirit [of the congregation] may be saved." (1 Cor. 5:5, 11-13) Paul also reported the disfellowshipping of others who had rebelled against the truth in the first century.—1 Tim. 1:20.

When a judicial committee concludes that an unrepentant wrongdoer should be disfellowshipped, it should let him know of the decision, clearly stating the Scriptural reason(s) for the disfellowshipping. When informing the wrongdoer of their decision, the judicial committee should tell him that if he believes that a serious error in judgment has been made and he wishes to appeal the decision, he may do so by writing a letter clearly stating the reasons for his appeal. He will be allowed seven days for this, from the time he was notified of the committee's decision. If such written appeal is received, the body of elders should contact the circuit overseer, who will designate elders to serve on an appeal committee to rehear the case. The elders selected to care for this weighty responsibility should be men who are experienced and qualified. Every effort should be made to conduct the appeal hearing within one week after the written appeal is received. If there is an appeal, announcement of the disfellowshipping will be held in abeyance. In the meantime, the accused person will be restricted from commenting and praying at meetings or from special privileges of service.

An appeal is granted as a kindness to the accused and allows him a further hearing of his concerns. Thus, if he deliberately fails to appear at the appeal hearing, the disfellowshipping should be announced after reasonable efforts have been made to contact him.

If the wrongdoer does not wish to appeal, the judicial committee should explain to him the need for repentance and what steps he can take toward being reinstated in due time. This would be both helpful and kind and should be done in the hope that he will change his ways and in time qualify to return to Jehovah's organization.—2 Cor. 2:6, 7.

ANNOUNCEMENT OF DISFELLOWSHIPPING

When it is necessary to disfellowship an unrepentant wrongdoer from the congregation, a brief announcement is made, simply stating: "[Name of person] is no longer one of Jehovah's Witnesses." There is no need to elaborate. This will alert faithful members of the congregation to stop associating with that person. (1 Cor. 5:11) The presiding overseer should approve this announcement.

DISASSOCIATION

The term "disassociation" applies to the action taken by a person who, although a baptized member of the congregation, deliberately repudiates his Christian standing, rejecting the congregation by his actions or by stating that he no longer wants to be recognized as or known as one of Jehovah's Witnesses. Because he is disassociated, his situation before Jehovah is far different from that of an inactive Christian, one who no longer shares in the field ministry. An inactive person may have failed to study God's Word regularly, or because of experiencing personal problems or persecution, he may have lost his zeal for serving Jehovah. The elders as well as other concerned members of the congregation will continue rendering appropriate spiritual assistance to an inactive brother. (Rom. 15:1; 1 Thess. 5:14; Heb. 12:12) However, the person who disassociates himself by repudiating the faith and deliberately abandoning Jehovah's worship is viewed in the same way as one who is disfellowshipped. A brief announcement is made to inform the congregation, stating: "[Name of person] is no longer one of Jehovah's Witnesses."

Concerning those who renounced their Christian faith in his day, the apostle John wrote: "They went out from us, but they were not of our sort; for if they had been of our sort, they would have remained with us." (1 John 2:19) For example, a person might renounce his place in the Christian congregation by his actions, such as by becoming part of a secular organization that has objectives contrary to the Bible and, hence, is under judgment by Jehovah God. (Isa. 2:4; Rev. 19:17-21) If a person who is a Christian chooses to join those who are disapproved by God, a brief announcement is made to the congregation, stating: "[Name of person] is no longer one of Jehovah's Witnesses." Such a person is treated in the same way as a disfellowshipped person. The presiding overseer should approve this announcement.

REINSTATEMENT

A disfellowshipped person may be reinstated when he gives clear evidence of repentance, demonstrating over a reasonable period of time that he has abandoned his sinful course and is desirous of having a good relationship with Jehovah and His organization. The elders are careful to allow sufficient time, perhaps many months, a year, or even longer, for the disfellowshipped person to prove that his repentance is genuine. When the body of elders receives a written plea for reinstatement, the judicial committee that disfellowshipped the person should, if possible, be the committee that speaks with the individual. The committee will evaluate the evidence of works of godly repentance on his part and decide whether to reinstate him at that time or not.

If the person requesting reinstatement was disfellowshipped by another congregation, a local judicial committee may meet with the person and consider the plea. Thereafter, the local judicial committee will communicate with the body of elders of the congregation that disfellowshipped the individual, giving them its recommendation. The involved committees will work together in unity to ensure that all the facts are gathered and a just decision is made. However, the decision to reinstate is made by the original judicial committee of the congregation that took the disfellowshipping action. If some members of the original committee are no longer in the congregation or qualified to serve, other elders from the original congregation can be chosen to replace them.

When the judicial committee is convinced that the disfellowshipped person is genuinely repentant and should be reinstated, an announcement of the reinstatement is made in the congregation where the individual was disfellowshipped. If the person is now in another congregation, the announcement will be made there as well. It should simply state: "[Name of person] is reinstated as one of Jehovah's Witnesses."

WHEN UNBAPTIZED PUBLISHERS ARE WRONGDOERS

What of unbaptized publishers who become involved in serious wrongdoing? Since they are not baptized members of the congregation, they cannot be formally disfellowshipped. However, they may not fully understand the Bible's standards, and kind counsel may help them to make straight paths for their feet.

If an unbaptized wrongdoer is unrepentant after two elders have met with him and have tried to help him, then it is necessary to inform the congregation. A brief announcement is made, stating: "[Name of person] is no longer recognized as an unbaptized publisher." The congregation will then view the wrongdoer as a person of the world. Although the offender is not disfellowshipped, Christians exercise caution with regard to any association with him. (1 Cor. 15:33) No field service reports would be accepted from him.

In time, an unbaptized person (adult or minor) who was removed as a publisher may wish to renew his association with the congregation and become a publisher again. In that situation, two elders would meet with him and ascertain his spiritual progress. If he has a good attitude, a Bible study may be held with him. If he progresses spiritually and eventually qualifies, a brief announcement can be made, stating: "[Name of person] is again recognized as an unbaptized publisher."

CASES INVOLVING MINOR BAPTIZED CHILDREN

Serious wrongdoing on the part of minor children who are baptized should be reported to the elders. When the elders handle cases of serious sins involving a minor, it is preferable that the baptized parents of the young person be present and cooperate with the judicial committee, not attempting to shield the erring child from necessary disciplinary action. Just as in dealing with adult offenders, the judicial committee endeavors to reprove and restore the wrongdoer. However, if the young person is unrepentant, disfellowshipping action is taken.

JEHOVAH BLESSES UNITED, CLEAN WORSHIP

All who are associated with the congregation of God today can certainly rejoice in the rich spiritual estate that Jehovah has given to his people. Our spiritual pastures have indeed been made lush, and we have been provided with an abundance of refreshing waters of truth. We have experienced Jehovah's protective care through his theocratic arrangement under the headship of Christ. (Ps., 23; Isa. 32:1, 2) Being in the spiritual paradise in these troublesome last days has given us a feeling of security.

By maintaining fine conduct and Christian unity as ministers of God's good news, we will continue to let the light of Kingdom truth shine forth. (Matt. 5:16) With Jehovah's blessing, we will have the joy of seeing many more people come to know Jehovah and serve with us in doing God's will.

CHAPTER 15

BENEFITING FROM THEOCRATIC SUBJECTION

BEING in subjection to God, the Universal Sovereign, is essential if we are to be organized to do Jehovah's will. Our recognizing his Son's headship over the Christian congregation is also necessary. And it is important that we observe the headship principle in other areas of life. Such theocratic subjection benefits everyone concerned.

The idea of subjection to constituted authority was introduced to mankind in the garden of Eden. It is embodied in God's commands found at Genesis 1:28 and 2:16, 17. Lower creatures were to be in subjection to humans, and Adam and Eve were to submit to God's will and authority. Obedience to this divine authority would result in peace and good order. The headship principle is later highlighted at 1 Corinthians 11:3. The apostle Paul wrote: "I want you to know that the head of every man is the Christ; in turn the head of a woman is the man; in turn the head of the Christ is God." So this indicates that other than Jehovah, everyone is subject to headship in this overall arrangement.

Most people today do not recognize or observe the headship principle. Why? The trouble started in Eden when mankind's parents deliberately chose to take themselves out from under God's sovereign headship. (Gen. 3:4, 5) However, they did not attain to greater freedom. Instead, they became subject to a wicked spirit creature, Satan the Devil. The first rebellion alienated mankind from God. (Col. 1:21) As a result, today the majority of mankind remain in the power of the wicked one.—1 John 5:19.

By learning the truth of God's Word and acting upon it, we have come out from under Satan's influence. As dedicated, baptized Witnesses, do we not accept Jehovah as the Sovereign of our life? Do we not agree with loyal King David, who acknowledged Jehovah as "head over all"? (1 Chron. 29:11) Certainly we do! We humbly confess: "Jehovah is God. It is he that has made us, and not we ourselves. We are his people and the sheep of his pasturage." (Ps. 100:3) We recognize Jehovah's greatness and his worthiness of total submission, since he created all things. (Rev. 4:11) As ministers of the true God, we follow Jesus Christ, who set the perfect example of subjection to God.

What did Jesus learn by the things he suffered while on earth? Hebrews 5:8 answers: "Although he was a Son, he learned obedience from the things he suffered." Yes, Jesus remained in loyal subjection to his heavenly Father even under adversity. Furthermore, Jesus did not do a single thing of his own initiative; he did not speak of his own originality, nor did he seek his own glory. (John 5:19, 30; 6:38; 7:16-18) During his ministry, he found delight in doing his Father's will, even though this course brought opposition and persecution. (John 15:20) Nonetheless, Jesus showed subjection to God by 'humbling himself' even to the point of "death on a torture stake." The outcome of his complete subjection to Jehovah was rewarding in many ways, resulting in everlasting salvation for mankind, exaltation for himself, and glory to his Father.—Phil. 2:5-11; Heb. 5:9.

AREAS OF THEOCRATIC SUBJECTION

Because Jehovah is the Universal Sovereign, we owe him our total subjection. (Isa. 33:22) Briefly reflecting on our everyday life as Jehovah's dedicated worshipers should make this evident. By putting God first in our life, doing his will, we are directed in the right way. (Ps. 16:8) We escape many of the anxieties and frustrations that overtake those who refuse to submit to Jehovah's sovereignty. Our Adversary, the Devil, constantly seeks to ensnare and devour us. We will experience deliverance from that wicked one provided we take a stand against him and humble ourselves before Jehovah in willing subjection. —Matt. 6:10, 13; 1 Pet. 5:6-9.

The benefits of subjecting ourselves to God extend to our relationships with others, which are measurably improved. We are spared problems that beset those who reflect this world's spirit of independence. Thanks to Jehovah God, we enjoy a happy marriage and family life as well as better relationships with fellow workers and employers. We conduct ourselves lawfully and with a good conscience toward governmental authorities. We also have the best associates, our Christian brothers.

Within the Christian congregation, we recognize Christ's headship and the authority he has given to the faithful and discreet slave class. This affects our attitude and conduct toward one another. Godly subjection in the congregation will move us to be obedient to God's Word in all aspects of our worship. This includes our ministry, meeting attendance and participation, relationship with the elders, and cooperation with organizational arrangements.—Matt. 24:45-47; 28:19, 20; Heb. 10:24, 25; 13:7, 17.

Our subjection to God allows us to enjoy the peaceful security of theocratic order. Such theocratic order is not oppressive. (1 John 5:3) Jehovah's divine qualities are reflected in the harmonious society of his godly subjects. (1 Cor. 14:33, 40) Our own observations and our experience with Jehovah's organization have led us to express sentiments similar to those of God's servant David. After noting the contrast between Jehovah's servants and the wicked, who boast in their own power and riches, David joyfully exclaimed: "Happy is the people whose God is Jehovah!" —Ps. 144:15.

Within marriage and the family structure, "the head of a woman is the man." At the same time, men are to be in subjection to Christ, while the Head of Christ is God. (1 Cor. 11:3) Wives are to be in subjection to their husbands, and children, to their parents. (Eph. 5:22-24; 6:1) Peace results when each family member follows the headship principle.

This requires that husbands exercise headship in a loving way, imitating Christ. (Eph. 5:25-29) When they do not abuse or abdicate their headship, it is a delight for the wife and the children to be in subjection. The wife's role is that of a helper, or complement. (Gen. 2:18) By patiently supporting and respecting her husband, she gains his favor and brings praise to God. (1 Pet. 3:1-4) When husbands and wives follow the Bible's counsel on headship, they set an example for their children in showing subjection to God.

Our being in subjection to God also affects how we view "the superior authorities," which have been "placed in their relative positions by God." (Rom. 13:1-7) As law-abiding citizens, Christians pay taxes; they pay back "Caesar's things to Caesar, but God's things to God." (Matt. 22:21) Being submissive and obedient to the duly constituted authorities in everything that is not in conflict with Jehovah's righteous law, we are able to direct our efforts, applying our energies to the important work of preaching the good news of God's established Kingdom.—Mark 13:10; Acts 5:29.

By adhering to Bible principles, Christians seek to improve their employer-employee relationships. Even though at times this may be difficult, servants of God strive to be at peace with all men. They serve honestly and reliably at their secular jobs. (Rom. 12:18; 1 Pet. 2:18) Thus, they do not become involved in controversies or violate their Bible-trained conscience.

Theocratic subjection affects all aspects of life. With eyes of faith, we see the day when all mankind will be subject to Jehovah God. (1 Cor. 15:27, 28) How blessed and favored those who joyfully acknowledge Jehovah's sovereignty will be, as they remain in subjection to him for all eternity!

CHAPTER 16

A UNITED BROTHERHOOD

AFTER dealing with one man, Abraham, and his descendants the Israelites exclusively for some 2,000 years, Jehovah God "turned his attention to the nations to take out of them a people for his name." (Acts 15:14) People for Jehovah's name would be his witnesses, gathered in unity of thought and action regardless of their physical location on earth. This uniting of a people for God's name would result from the fulfillment of the commission that Jesus gave to his followers. He said: "Go therefore and make disciples of people of all the nations, baptizing them in the name of the Father and of the Son and of the holy spirit, teaching them to observe all the things I have commanded you."—Matt. 28:19, 20.

By dedicating yourself to Jehovah and being baptized, you have become a disciple of Jesus Christ and are now part of a united, worldwide brotherhood of Christians, who do not allow national, tribal, or economic differences to divide them. (Ps. 133:1) As a result, you love and respect your Christian companions in the congregation, even though some of them may be of a different race or nationality. It may well be that some of your closest companions in the congregation would formerly have been socially unacceptable to you because of basic racial, cultural, educational, or economic differences. Unitedly, we share unhypocritical brotherly love that forms an unbreakable bond far stronger than any other relationship, whether social, religious, or family.—Mark 10:29, 30; Col. 3:14; 1 Pet. 1:22.

ADJUSTMENTS IN THINKING

If some have difficulty breaking free from racial, political, social, or other ingrained prejudices, they might think of the early Jewish Christians, who had to break free from Jewish religious prejudices against people of all other nations. Recall that when Peter was instructed to go to the home of the Roman centurion Cornelius, Jehovah kindly prepared Peter for the assignment. Please read the entire account at Acts chapter 10.

In a vision, Peter was told to kill and eat certain animals that were ceremonially unclean for Jews even to touch. When Peter objected, a voice from heaven told him: "You stop calling defiled the things God has cleansed." (Acts 10:15) It took this divine intervention for Peter to condition his mind for the assignment he was about to receive, namely, to go and visit a man of the nations. But when obeying Jehovah's direction, Peter declared to those gathered: "You well know how unlawful it is for a Jew to join himself to or approach a man of another race; and yet God has shown me I should call no man defiled or unclean. Hence I came, really without objection, when I was sent for." (Acts 10:28, 29) Thereafter, Peter witnessed the evidence of Jehovah's approval of Cornelius and his household.

Saul of Tarsus, a highly educated Pharisee, had to humble himself and associate with those who had formerly been socially unacceptable to him. He even had to take direction from them. (Acts 4:13; Gal. 1:13-20; Phil. 3:4-11) We can only imagine the adjustments that must have taken place in the thinking of such people as Sergius Paulus, Dionysius, Damaris, Philemon, Onesimus, and others as they accepted the good news and became disciples of Jesus Christ. —Acts 13:6-12; 17:22, 33, 34; Philem. 8-20.

MAINTAINING OUR INTERNATIONAL UNITY

No doubt the love of the brothers and sisters in your congregation helped draw you to Jehovah and his organization. You had not experienced such love with other groups. You observed the unmistakable mark of love and unity that characterizes true disciples of Jesus Christ, as he expressed: "I am giving you a new commandment, that you love one another; just as I have loved you, that you also love one another. By this all will know that you are my disciples, if you have love among yourselves." (John 13:34, 35) But then how much more you came to appreciate

Jehovah's dealings with mankind today when you realized that the love in your congregation is only a taste of the love that exists in the worldwide association of Jehovah's people! You are a witness to and a part of the fulfillment of Bible prophecy about the gathering of people in the last days to worship Jehovah in peace and unity. Why not read that prophecy? It is found at Micah 4:1-5.

In view of the many divisive factors that exist today, who would ever have thought it possible to unite people "out of all nations and tribes and peoples and tongues"? (Rev. 7:9) Consider the differences between the people of a high-technology society and those who hold to ancient tribal customs. Look at the religious rivalries among people of the same race and nationality. With nationalism coming to the fore, people have become more divided politically than ever before. And then if you consider the vast economic differences between groups of people everywhere along with countless other divisive factors, the uniting of individuals out of all these nations, factions, groups, and classes in an unbreakable bond of love and peace is a miracle that could be performed only by Almighty God.—Zech. 4:6.

But such unity is a reality, and when you became a dedicated, baptized Witness of Jehovah, you became part of it. Your faith has brought you into a spiritual paradise. Benefiting from that paradise, you have the responsibility to help maintain it. This is done by heeding the apostle Paul's words found at Galatians 6:10: "As long as we have time favorable for it, let us work what is good toward all, but especially toward those related to us in the faith." Maintaining the spiritual paradise also means "doing nothing out of contentiousness or out of egotism, but with lowliness of mind considering that the others are superior to you, keeping an eye, not in personal interest upon just your own matters, but also in personal interest upon those of the others." (Phil. 2:3, 4) As long as we train ourselves to see our Christian brothers and sisters as Jehovah sees them and not according to what they are in the flesh—not fixing attention on human imperfection that will eventually disappear—we will continue to enjoy peaceful and happy relationships with them.—Eph. 4:23, 24.

CONCERN FOR ONE ANOTHER

As the apostle Paul illustrated so well, members of the congregation belong to one another and care for one another. (1 Cor. 12:14-26) What affects one part, or segment, of the organization affects all of God's people. We may be separated by great distances from some of the members of the worldwide brotherhood, but we are not less concerned about their welfare. If some of our brothers are being persecuted, the rest of us are greatly distressed. If some are suffering want or have become victims of disaster or war or civil strife, the rest are eager to find ways to render spiritual as well as material assistance.—2 Cor. 1:8-11.

All of us should pray for our brothers every day. There are brothers who are facing temptations to do what is bad. The sufferings of some of our brothers may be publicly known, but the opposition that others face daily from workmates and from within divided households is relatively unknown. (Matt. 10:35, 36; 1 Thess. 2:14) This is a concern of all because we are a worldwide association of brothers. (1 Pet. 5:9) There are also those working hard in Jehovah's service, taking the lead in the preaching work and in overseeing congregations. And there are those charged with the oversight of the worldwide work. All need our prayers, by which we demonstrate our genuine interest in our brothers and the love we have for them, even when there may not be anything else that we can personally do to be of assistance.—Eph. 1:16; 1 Thess. 1:2, 3; 5:25.

With all the turmoil on earth during these last days and the resulting emergencies as well as frequent disasters, such as earthquakes and floods, Christian Witnesses of Jehovah must be prepared to come to the aid of one another. At times, this may mean conducting extensive relief efforts and arranging for large amounts of material assistance. First-century Christians set a fine example in this regard. Remembering Jesus' counsel, the disciples in other lands gladly sent material gifts to the brothers in Judea during a time of famine. (Acts 11:27-30; 20:35) The apostle Paul organized relief ministration so that everything was carried out in an orderly manner. (2 Cor. 9:1-15) In modern times, when our brothers become victims of circumstances and need material relief, the organization and individual Christians are quick to respond and supply what is needed.

SET APART TO DO JEHOVAH'S WILL

Our united, worldwide brotherhood is organized to do Jehovah's will. At this particular time, his will is that the good news of the Kingdom be preached in all the earth for a witness to all the nations. (Matt. 24:14) While we are doing this work, it is Jehovah's will that we always conduct ourselves in accord with his high moral standards. (1 Pet. 1:14-16) In order to get Jehovah's work done, all of us should be willing to subject ourselves to one another and to work for the advancement of the good news. (Eph. 5:21) As never before, this is, not a time to seek our own personal interests, but a time to put God's Kingdom first in our life. (Matt. 6:33) Keeping this in mind and working in unity with one another for the sake of the good news bring joyful satisfaction now and will lead to everlasting blessings.

As Jehovah's Witnesses, we are truly unique, set apart from the rest of mankind as a clean people, zealous in service to our God. (Titus 2:14) We are not distinct and separate simply to call attention to ourselves. Rather, our worship of Jehovah makes us different. Not only do we work shoulder to shoulder with our brothers around the earth but we even speak the one language of truth and unitedly act in harmony with the truth we speak. This was foretold when Jehovah declared through his prophet Zephaniah: "I shall give to peoples the change to a pure language, in order for them all to call upon the name of Jehovah, in order to serve him shoulder to shoulder." —Zeph. 3:9.

Then Jehovah inspired Zephaniah to describe the united, clean, worldwide brotherhood that has become a reality today: "As regards the remaining ones of Israel, they will do no unrighteousness, nor speak a lie, nor will there be found in their mouths a tricky tongue; for they themselves will feed and actually lie stretched out, and there will be no one making them tremble." (Zeph. 3:13) Having gained an understanding of Jehovah's Word of truth and made over their mind and conformed their way of life to Jehovah's standards, Jehovah's Witnesses are able to work in unity. They accomplish what appears to be impossible in the eyes of those who view matters from a human standpoint. Yes, the worldwide Christian association is indeed a distinct people, God's people, bringing honor to him in all the earth.—Mic. 2:12.

The worldwide association of Jehovah's Witnesses exemplifies what Jesus commanded and what he pointed out as the sure identifying mark of his true disciples. Those seeking to know Jehovah have this convincing evidence before them as they observe what is taking place among his people. How happy we are to be a part of Jehovah's organized people, who have the privilege of carrying on a glorious ministry in this time of the end! By continuing to clothe ourselves with love and identifying ourselves with this distinguishing mark, we can be confident that we will have many joyous privileges of service within our united, worldwide brotherhood.

CHAPTER 17

STAY CLOSE TO JEHOVAH'S ORGANIZATION

THE disciple James wrote: "Draw close to God, and he will draw close to you." (Jas. 4:8) Yes, Jehovah is neither too lofty nor too far removed to hear our expressions to him, despite our imperfections. (Acts 17:27) If we take steps to draw close to God, he will draw close to us. We do this by building a close personal relationship with Jehovah that includes earnest communication with him in prayer. (Ps. 39:12) We also cultivate intimacy with God through a regular study of his Word, the Bible. With accurate knowledge and understanding, we get to know Jehovah God, his purposes, and his will for us. (2 Tim. 3:16, 17) In turn, we learn to love Jehovah and develop a wholesome fear of displeasing him.—Ps. 25:14.

Closeness with Jehovah, however, is possible only through his Son, Jesus. (John 17:3; Rom. 5:10) No human could ever give us better insight into the mind of Jehovah God than Jesus did. He was so intimately acquainted with his Father that he could say: "Who the Son is no one knows but the Father; and who the Father is, no one knows but the Son, and he to whom the Son is willing to reveal him." (Luke 10:22) So when we study what the Gospels reveal about the way Jesus thought and felt, we are, in effect, learning how Jehovah thinks and feels. Such knowledge enables us to draw closer to our God.

Under the headship of God's Son, we cultivate intimacy with Jehovah by staying close to the modern visible channel that helps us learn how to do God's will. As foretold at Matthew 24:45-47, the Master, Jesus Christ, has appointed "the faithful and discreet slave," made up of anointed Christians on earth, to provide "food at the proper time" for the household of faith. Today, this "slave" supplies us with an abundance of spiritual food in the form of Bible study aids. Through this channel, Jehovah counsels us to read his Word daily, to attend our Christian meetings regularly, and to have a meaningful share in preaching the "good news of the kingdom." (Matt. 24:14; 28:19, 20; Josh. 1:8; Ps. 1:1-3) Never would we want to have a fleshly viewpoint of this channel of communication. To do so could cause us to lose sight of the fact that Jehovah is directing his organization, and we could thereby reject his efforts to draw us closer to him. Instead, we should endeavor to stay close to the visible part of Jehovah's organization and to respond to its direction. This will draw us closer to our God, Jehovah, and will serve to strengthen and protect us despite trials.

WHY TRIALS ARE INCREASING

It may be that you have been in the truth for many years, and if so, you certainly know what it means to endure tests of integrity. Even if you have come to know Jehovah and associate with his people for only a short period of time, you too can testify to the fact that Satan the Devil opposes anyone who submits to Jehovah's sovereignty. (2 Tim. 3:12) But whether you have endured little or much, there is no reason for you to become fearful or discouraged, since you have Jehovah's sure promise that he will sustain you and reward your endurance with deliverance and future life.—Heb. 13:5, 6; Rev. 2:10.

All of us may yet be subjected to particularly difficult trials during these remaining days of Satan's system. Ever since the war in heaven that followed the establishment of God's Kingdom in 1914, Satan has not been permitted access to Jehovah's heavens. He was hurled down to the earth, where he and his wicked angels have been confined since that time. The increased woe on the earth since 1914, including the intensified persecution of Jehovah's dedicated servants, is a result of Satan's anger and is proof that we are living in the last days of his wicked rule over mankind.—Rev. 12:1-12.

Infuriated by his debased condition, Satan knows that his time is short. With the aid of his demons, he makes every effort to interfere with the preaching and teaching work of Jehovah's people and to destroy our unity. This puts Jehovah's servants at the battle lines of the spiritual warfare described at Ephesians 6:12 as "a wrestling, not against blood and flesh, but against the governments, against the authorities, against the world rulers of this darkness, against the wicked spirit forces in the heavenly places." That warfare will culminate in the great tribulation, now near at hand. If we are to come off victorious, on Jehovah's side, we must, not let up in the fight, but keep our spiritual armor intact and push ahead in the all-out war against every wicked machination of the Devil. (Eph. 6:10-17) This calls for endurance on our part as we keep on in the ministry entrusted to our care. But just what is involved in this, and how will we be able to endure?

CULTIVATING ENDURANCE

Endurance means "the ability to withstand hardship, adversity, or stress." In a spiritual sense, it refers to the quality of firmness in doing what is right in the face of hardship, opposition, persecution, or other factors designed to turn us away from our determined course of integrity to God. Christian endurance must be cultivated. This takes time. Our ability to endure increases as we make spiritual progress. By enduring minor tests of our faith from the very beginning of our Christian course and by remaining firm in our dedication, we become stronger, able to endure more difficult trials that are sure to come. We cannot afford to wait until major trials come along before making it our determination to stand firm in the faith. Our firm decision must be made before the test comes. Pointing out that endurance is to be cultivated along with other godly qualities, the apostle Peter wrote: "By your contributing in response all earnest effort, supply to your faith virtue, to your virtue knowledge, to your knowledge self-control, to your self-control endurance, to your endurance godly devotion, to your godly devotion brotherly affection, to your brotherly affection love."—2 Pet. 1:5-7; 1 Tim. 6:11.

The importance of cultivating endurance is called to our attention by what James wrote: "Consider it all joy, my brothers, when you meet with various trials, knowing as you do that this tested quality of your faith works out endurance. But let endurance have its work complete, that you may be complete and sound in all respects, not lacking in anything." (Jas. 1:2-4) James says that Christians should welcome trials and be joyful about them because they help us to work out endurance. Have you looked at matters that way? Then James shows that endurance itself has a work to perform in perfecting our Christian personality and in making us fully acceptable to God. Yes, our endurance is built up day by day as we face and overcome trials large and small. Endurance, in turn, produces other desirable qualities that we need. If we beg off from enduring minor trials that come along, we may not be able to face larger, more important tests of our faith.—Luke 16:10.

Our endurance is pleasing to Jehovah; it will move him to grant us the reward of everlasting life. James further stated: "Happy is the man that keeps on enduring trial, because on becoming approved he will receive the crown of life, which Jehovah promised to those who continue loving him." (Jas. 1:12) Yes, it is with life in view that we endure. Without endurance, we cannot stay in the truth. If we succumb to worldly pressures, we will be forced back into the world. Without endurance, we will not continue to have Jehovah's spirit and therefore cannot produce its fruitage in our life.

If we are to keep on enduring in these difficult times, we need to cultivate the proper attitude toward suffering as Christians. Recall that James wrote: "Consider it all joy." That may not be easy to do inasmuch as physical suffering or mental anguish may be involved. But remember that future life is at stake. An experience of the apostles helps us to see how we can rejoice in present sufferings. The account is found in the book of Acts and reads: "They summoned the apostles, flogged them, and ordered them to stop speaking upon the basis of Jesus' name, and let them go. These, therefore, went their way from before the Sanhedrin, rejoicing because they had been counted worthy to be dishonored in behalf of his name." (Acts 5:40, 41) They understood that their suffering was proof that they had been obedient to Jesus' command and that they had received Jehovah's approval. Years later, when writing his first inspired letter, Peter commented on the value of such suffering for righteousness' sake. Please read what he had to say, at 1 Peter 4:12-16.

Another experience involves Paul and Silas. When carrying on their missionary work in Philippi, they were arrested and charged with disturbing the city and publishing unlawful customs. As a result, they were severely beaten and thrown into prison. The Bible account tells us that while they were yet in prison with their wounds unattended, "about the middle of the night Paul and Silas were praying and praising God with song; yes, the prisoners were hearing them." (Acts 16:16-25) Paul and his companion rightly viewed their sufferings for Christ not only as evidence of their own integrity before God and men but also as a means of giving a further witness to those who might be inclined to listen to the good news. The life of others was involved. Later the jailer and his household listened and became disciples. (Acts 16:26-34) Paul and Silas trusted in Jehovah, in his power, and in his willingness to sustain them in their sufferings. They were not disappointed.

Today, too, Jehovah has provided all that we need to sustain us during times of trial. He wants us to endure. He has given us his inspired Word to equip us with accurate knowledge concerning his purpose. This builds up our faith. We have the opportunity to associate with fellow believers, to study God's Word, and to perform our sacred service. We also have the privilege of maintaining close association with Jehovah himself, through prayer. He listens to our expressions of praise and our earnest requests for help in keeping a clean standing before him. (Phil. 4:13) And not to be overlooked is the strength derived from contemplating the hope set before us.—Matt. 24:13; Rev. 21:1-4.

ENDURING VARIOUS TRIALS

The trials we face today are much like those faced by the early disciples of Jesus Christ. In modern times Jehovah's Witnesses have suffered verbal and physical abuse at the hands of misinformed opposers. Just as in the days of the apostles, much of the opposition is instigated by fanatic religious elements whose false teachings and practices are exposed by the Kingdom good news. (Acts 17:5-9, 13) At times, Jehovah's people have found relief by claiming legal rights that are guaranteed by political governments. (Acts 22:25; 25:11) However, rulers themselves have also imposed official bans on our work, endeavoring to put an end to our Christian ministry. (Ps. 2:1-3) Under such circumstances, we boldly follow the example of the faithful apostles and continue to "obey God as ruler rather than men."—Acts 5:29.

As the spirit of nationalism continues to grow throughout the earth, greater pressures are brought to bear upon preachers of the good news to abandon their God-given ministry. All of God's servants appreciate more fully the warning found at Revelation 14:9-12 concerning the worship of "the wild beast and its image." We realize the significance of John's words: "Here is where it means endurance for the holy ones, those who observe the commandments of God and the faith of Jesus."

Tests that come because of wars, revolutions, or outright persecution and official bans may make it impossible for you to carry on Christian worship openly. Circumstances may develop making it impossible to hold large congregation meetings. Contact with the branch office may temporarily be broken off. Visits by circuit overseers may be interrupted. New publications may not arrive. If any of these things happen, what should you do?

The answer is: Do whatever you can and as much as you can in the way of pure worship, under the circumstances. Personal study should be possible. Usually small groups can meet for study in homes. Publications studied in the past and the Bible itself can be used as a basis for meetings. Do not become excited or worried. Generally, the Governing Body will be able to establish some form of communication with responsible brothers in a short time.

But even if you find yourself isolated from all your Christian brothers, keep in mind that you are not isolated from Jehovah and his Son, Jesus Christ. Your hope can remain firm. Jehovah can still hear your prayers, and he can strengthen you with his spirit. Look to him for guidance. Remember that you are a servant of Jehovah and a disciple of Jesus Christ, so as opportunities to witness open up, make good use of them. Jehovah will bless your efforts, and others may soon join you in true worship.—Acts 4:13-31; 5: 27-42; Phil. 1:27-30; 4:6, 7; 2 Tim. 4:16-18.

Even if, like the apostles and others, you are faced with the very threat of death, put your trust in "the God who raises up the dead." (2 Cor. 1:8-10) Your faith in his provision of the resurrection can help you to endure even the most severe opposition. (Luke 21: 19) Christ Jesus set the example; he knew that his faithfulness under test would strengthen others to endure. You can be a source of strength to your brothers in a similar way.—John 16:33; Heb. 12:2, 3; 1 Pet. 2:21.

Besides persecution and direct opposition to our ministry, there are other difficult situations that you may have to endure. Although having the freedom to preach openly, some have become discouraged and have stopped serving Jehovah because of the apathy of people in their territory. Others have had to cope with their own physical or emotional illnesses or otherwise have had to endure limitations imposed by their human frailties. The apostle Paul had to endure a trial of some sort that interfered with his service or made it difficult at times. (2 Cor. 12:7) Also, Epaphroditus, a first-century Christian from Philippi, became "depressed because [his friends] heard he had fallen sick." (Phil. 2:25-27) Our human imperfections and those of others may pose problems particularly difficult to endure. Imperfections may show up as personality conflicts with fellow Christians. But such obstacles too can be successfully endured and overcome by those who adhere to the counsel of Jehovah's Word.—Ezek. 2:3-5; 1 Cor. 9:27; 13:8; Col. 3:12-14; 1 Pet. 4:8.

DETERMINED TO REMAIN FAITHFUL

We must always hold fast to the one whom Jehovah has appointed as Head of the congregation, Christ Jesus. (Col. 2:18, 19) We need to work closely with "the faithful and discreet slave" and those appointed as overseers. (Heb. 13:7, 17) By adhering closely to theocratic arrangements and cooperating with those taking the lead, we will be well organized to do Jehovah's will. We need to make full use of the privilege of prayer. Remember, not even prison walls or solitary confinement can cut off our communication with our loving heavenly Father or disrupt the unity we have with fellow worshipers.

With determination and endurance, let us do all that we can to carry out our commission to preach, persevering in the work that the resurrected Jesus Christ set out for his followers to do: "Go therefore and make disciples of people of all the nations, baptizing them in the name of the Father and of the Son and of the holy spirit, teaching them to observe all the things I have commanded you." (Matt. 28:19, 20) Like Jesus, let us endure and keep the Kingdom hope and the prospect of everlasting life clearly before us. (Heb. 12:2) As baptized disciples of Christ, we have the privilege of sharing in the fulfillment of Jesus' prophecy regarding "the conclusion of the system of things." He said: "This good news of the kingdom will be preached in all the inhabited earth for a witness to all the nations; and then the end will come." (Matt. 24:3, 14) If we apply ourselves wholeheartedly to that work during this time, we will experience the joy of entering into an eternity of life in Jehovah's righteous new world!

APPENDIX

A Message to the Unbaptized Publisher:

It is a fine privilege to serve with the congregation as an unbaptized publisher. You are to be commended for the spiritual progress you have made. You have taken in accurate knowledge through a study of God's Word and have exercised faith on the basis of that knowledge.—John 17:3; Heb. 11:6.

It may be that before you started to study with Jehovah's Witnesses, you were associated in some way with a different religious organization. Or you may have engaged in other activity out of harmony with Bible principles. But now you have manifested your faith by repentance, which means a deep regret over past involvements or wrongdoing. You have also manifested your faith by conversion, which means rejecting a former wrong course and determining to do what is right in God's sight.—Acts 3:19.

On the other hand, it may be that you were blessed with being raised, taught, and trained as part of a Christian household. Perhaps like Timothy, "from infancy you have known the holy writings," and you have thereby been safeguarded from involvement in unchristian conduct and serious wrongdoing. (2 Tim. 3:15) You have learned to resist peer pressure and other inducements to engage in what is bad in Jehovah's eyes. You have demonstrated faith by maintaining steadfastness for right worship and by sharing Christian beliefs with others. You have been trained in the Christian ministry by accompanying your parents or others in the field service. Now you have made a personal decision to serve Jehovah as an unbaptized publisher with the congregation.

In either case, whether you have been instructed in Jehovah's ways from infancy or have come to know him later in life, you may now be contemplating two further steps in your spiritual progress—dedication and baptism. You make a dedication to Jehovah by approaching him in prayer and expressing your personal decision to give him exclusive devotion forever. (Matt. 16:24) In symbol of that dedication, you then undergo baptism by complete immersion in water. (Matt. 28:19, 20) Through dedication and baptism, you become an ordained minister of Jehovah God. What a wonderful privilege this is!

As your study of the Bible has indicated, though, this course of action will be met with various challenges. Remember, shortly after Jesus was baptized, he was "led by the spirit up into the wilderness to be tempted by the Devil." (Matt. 4:1) Following your baptism as a disciple of Christ, you can expect further tests. (John 15:20) They will come in various forms. You may face opposition from family. (Matt. 10:36) You may be ridiculed by workmates and former associates. But always remember Jesus' words found at Mark 10:29, 30: "Truly I say to you men, No one has left house or brothers or sisters or mother or father or children or fields for my sake and for the sake of the good news who will not get a hundredfold now in this period of time, houses and brothers and sisters and mothers and children and fields, with persecutions, and in the coming system of things everlasting life." So continue working hard to stay close to Jehovah and to live up to his righteous standards.

When you desire to be baptized, make this known to the elders in the congregation. The questions that follow this message provide the basis for discussions that the elders will have with you in order to determine whether you qualify for baptism. You may begin reviewing these questions privately as a part of your regular personal study program.

In preparation for these discussions, take time to read and reflect on the quoted and cited Scripture references. In many cases, they will not provide the complete answer to the question posed, but they will help you to see the Scriptural basis for an answer. If you are not sure of the answer to a question, you may find it helpful to do some additional research using the Bible and the publications provided by "the faithful and discreet slave." (Matt. 24:45) You may wish to make personal notes in this book and on a separate sheet of paper. You may use those notes and have this book open during your discussions with the elders. If you have difficulty understanding any of the questions, feel free to ask for assistance from the one who is studying the Bible with you or from the elders.

In your discussions with the elders, do not feel that you have to give lengthy or complicated answers to the questions. A simple, direct answer in your own words will usually suffice. For many of the questions, it is also beneficial to refer to one or two Bible texts that show the Scriptural basis for your answer.

If you have not yet gained sufficient knowledge of basic Bible teachings, the elders will arrange for you to receive assistance so that you will be able to express in your own words a proper understanding of the Scriptures and qualify to be baptized at a later time.

[Note to congregation elders: Instructions for handling discussions with baptism candidates appear on pages 217-18.]

QUESTIONS FOR THOSE DESIRING TO BE BAPTIZED

♦

PART I
ELEMENTARY BIBLE TEACHINGS

Unless you were raised by Christian parents, your study of the Bible with Jehovah's Witnesses has acquainted you with the pattern of truth, and very likely, you find that it is quite different from what you formerly believed. (2 Tim. 1:13) What you have learned has brought you great spiritual refreshment and has no doubt given you the hope of future life and blessings on a paradise earth under God's Kingdom. Your faith in God's Word has been strengthened, and through association with the Christian congregation, you have already experienced many blessings. You have come to appreciate how Jehovah is dealing with his people today.—Zech. 8:23.

Whether you were raised in a Christian household or not, as you prepare for water baptism in symbol of your personal dedication to Jehovah God, you will benefit from a review of elementary Bible teachings, conducted by the congregation elders. (Heb. 6:1-3) May Jehovah continue to bless all your endeavors to take in knowledge of him, and may he grant you the promised reward.—John 17:3.

1. Who is the true God?

You well know today, and you must call back to your heart that Jehovah is the true God in the heavens above and on the earth beneath. There is no other.—Deut. 4:39.

Even though there are those who are called "gods," whether in heaven or on earth, just as there are many "gods" and many "lords," there is actually to us one God the Father, out of whom all things are, and we for him; and there is one Lord, Jesus Christ, through whom all things are, and we through him.—1 Cor. 8:5, 6.

Additional references: Ps. 83:18; Isa. 43:10-12.

2. What are some of Jehovah's outstanding qualities?

God is *love*.—1 John 4:8.

The Rock, perfect is his activity, for all his ways are *justice*. A God of faithfulness, with whom there is no injustice; righteous and upright is he.—Deut. 32:4.

O the depth of God's riches and *wisdom* and knowledge! How unsearchable his judgments are and past tracing out his ways are!—Rom. 11:33.

Alas, O Sovereign Lord Jehovah! Here you yourself have made the heavens and the earth by your great *power* and by your outstretched arm. The whole matter is not too wonderful for you yourself.—Jer. 32:17.

3. What terms does the Bible use to help us understand some aspects of Jehovah's authority?

Jehovah is our Judge, Jehovah is our Statute-giver, Jehovah is our King; he himself will save us.—Isa. 33:22.

Have you not come to know or have you not heard? Jehovah, the Creator of the extremities of the earth, is a God to time indefinite. He does not tire out or grow weary. There is no searching out of his understanding.—Isa. 40:28.

4. What does it mean to give Jehovah exclusive devotion? Why does he alone deserve such devotion?

You must love Jehovah your God with your whole heart and with your whole soul and with your whole mind and with your whole strength.—Mark 12:30.

Jesus said to [Satan]: "It is written, 'It is Jehovah your God you must worship, and it is to him alone you must render sacred service.'"—Luke 4:8.

You are worthy, Jehovah, even our God, to receive the glory and the honor and the power, because you created all things, and because of your will they existed and were created.—Rev. 4:11.

Additional references: Ex. 20:4, 5; Acts 17:28.

5. How should we view and treat God's personal name?

I will exalt you, O my God the King, and I will bless your name to time indefinite, even forever. All day long I will bless you, and I will praise your name to time indefinite, even forever.—Ps. 145:1, 2.

You must pray, then, this way: "Our Father in the heavens, let your name be sanctified."—Matt. 6:9.

6. Why is it important for us to use God's personal name in worship?

Symeon has related thoroughly how God for the first time turned his attention to the nations to take out of them a people for his name.—Acts 15:14.

Everyone who calls on the name of Jehovah will be saved.—Rom. 10:13.

Additional references: Ex. 20:7; Ps. 91:14; Joel 2:32.

7. How will Jehovah God sanctify his name? How can we have a share in this?

I shall certainly magnify myself and sanctify myself and make myself known before the eyes of many nations; and they will have to know that I am Jehovah.—Ezek. 38:23.

O may they be ashamed and be disturbed for all times, and may they become abashed and perish; that people may know that you, whose name is Jehovah, you alone are the Most High over all the earth.—Ps. 83:17, 18.

Be wise, my son, and make my heart rejoice, that I may make a reply to him that is taunting me.—Prov. 27:11.

Additional references: Ezek. 36:16-18; 1 Pet. 2:12.

8. Why would it be wrong for us to make an image of God or to attempt to worship him through the use of images?

You must not make for yourself a carved image, any form like anything that is in the heavens above or that is on the earth underneath or that is in the waters under the earth. You must not bow down to them or be led to serve them, because I Jehovah your God am a God exacting exclusive devotion.—Deut. 5:8, 9.

I am Jehovah. That is my name; and to no one else shall I give my own glory, neither my praise to graven images. —Isa. 42:8.

God is a Spirit, and those worshiping him must worship with spirit and truth.—John 4:24.

We are walking by faith, not by sight.—2 Cor. 5:7.

9. What does it mean for a person to dedicate himself to Jehovah? Have you made your personal dedication to Jehovah in prayer?

Look! I am come (in the roll of the book it is written about me) to do your will, O God. . . . Look! I am come to do your will.—Heb. 10:7, 9.

Jesus said to his disciples: "If anyone wants to come after me, let him disown himself and pick up his torture stake and continually follow me."—Matt. 16:24.

10. Who is Jesus Christ?

Peter said: "You are the Christ, the Son of the living God."—Matt. 16:16.

He is the image of the invisible God, the firstborn of all creation; because by means of him all other things were created in the heavens and upon the earth, the things visible and the things invisible, no matter whether they are thrones or lordships or governments or authorities. All other things have been created through him and for him. —Col. 1:15, 16.

Additional references: John 1:1, 2, 14; Acts 2:36.

11. What is Jesus' position in relation to Jehovah God, and what authority has Jehovah given him?

I am going my way to the Father, because the Father is greater than I am.—John 14:28.

Keep this mental attitude in you that was also in Christ Jesus, who, although he was existing in God's form, gave no consideration to a seizure, namely, that he should be equal to God. No, but he emptied himself and took a slave's form and came to be in the likeness of men. More than that, when he found himself in fashion as a man, he humbled himself and became obedient as far as death, yes, death on a torture stake. For this very reason also God exalted him to a superior position and kindly gave him the name that is above every other name, so that in the name of Jesus every knee should bend of those in heaven and those on earth and those under the ground, and every tongue should openly acknowledge that Jesus Christ is Lord to the glory of God the Father.—Phil. 2:5-11.

Additional references: Dan. 7:13, 14; John 14:10, 11; 1 Cor. 11:3.

12. Why did Jesus come to earth and die a sacrificial death?

The Son of man came, not to be ministered to, but to minister and to give his soul a ransom in exchange for many. —Matt. 20:28.

God loved the world so much that he gave his only-begotten Son, in order that everyone exercising faith in him might not be destroyed but have everlasting life. —John 3:16.

He beheld Jesus coming toward him, and he said: "See, the Lamb of God that takes away the sin of the world!" —John 1:29.

13. Why do we need the ransom, and how does it affect you personally?

By means of him we have the release by ransom through the blood of that one, yes, the forgiveness of our trespasses.—Eph. 1:7.

The love the Christ has compels us, because this is what we have judged, that one man died for all; so, then, all had died; and he died for all that those who live might live no longer for themselves, but for him who died for them and was raised up.—2 Cor. 5:14, 15.

Additional references: Rom. 3:23; 1 John 4:11.

14. What is the holy spirit, and what has been accomplished by means of it?

God's active force was moving to and fro over the surface of the waters.—Gen. 1:2.

No prophecy of Scripture springs from any private interpretation. For prophecy was at no time brought by man's will, but men spoke from God as they were borne along by holy spirit.—2 Pet. 1:20, 21.

They all became filled with holy spirit and started to speak with different tongues, just as the spirit was granting them to make utterance.—Acts 2:4.

15. How does holy spirit operate for our benefit today?

You will receive power when the holy spirit arrives upon you, and you will be witnesses of me both in Jerusalem and in all Judea and Samaria and to the most distant part of the earth.—Acts 1:8.

Pay attention to yourselves and to all the flock, among which the holy spirit has appointed you overseers, to shepherd the congregation of God.—Acts 20:28.

It is to us God has revealed them through his spirit, for the spirit searches into all things, even the deep things of God.—1 Cor. 2:10.

The fruitage of the spirit is love, joy, peace, long-suffering, kindness, goodness, faith, mildness, self-control. Against such things there is no law.—Gal. 5: 22, 23.

Additional references: Matt. 10:19, 20; John 14:26.

16. What is the Kingdom of God?

In the days of those kings the God of heaven will set up a kingdom that will never be brought to ruin. And the kingdom itself will not be passed on to any other people. It will crush and put an end to all these kingdoms, and it itself will stand to times indefinite.—Dan. 2:44.

Let your kingdom come. Let your will take place, as in heaven, also upon earth.—Matt. 6:10.

Additional references: Isa. 9:7; John 18:36.

17. What blessings will Kingdom rule bring for the earth and for mankind?

He will wipe out every tear from their eyes, and death will be no more, neither will mourning nor outcry nor pain be anymore. The former things have passed away.—Rev. 21:4.

The sucking child will certainly play upon the hole of the cobra; and upon the light aperture of a poisonous snake will a weaned child actually put his own hand. They will not do any harm or cause any ruin in all my holy mountain.—Isa. 11:8, 9.

Additional references: Isa. 26:9; 65:21, 22.

18. What does it mean to seek first the Kingdom?

Stop storing up for yourselves treasures upon the earth . . . Rather, store up for yourselves treasures in heaven . . . No one can slave for two masters . . . You cannot slave for God and for Riches. . . . So never be anxious and say, "What are we to eat?" or, "What are we to drink?" or, "What are we to put on?" For all these are the things the nations are eagerly pursuing.—Matt. 6:19-32.

The kingdom of the heavens is like a treasure hidden in the field, which a man found and hid; and for the joy he has he goes and sells what things he has and buys that field. Again the kingdom of the heavens is like a traveling merchant seeking fine pearls. Upon finding one pearl of high value, away he went and promptly sold all the things he had and bought it.—Matt. 13:44-46.

Additional references: Matt. 16:24; 19:27-29.

19. How do we know that we have entered into the time of the end and that God's Kingdom is ruling?

While he was sitting upon the Mount of Olives, the disciples approached him privately, saying: "Tell us, When will these things be, and what will be the sign of your presence and of the conclusion of the system of things?"—Matt. 24:3.

Know this, that in the last days critical times hard to deal with will be here. For men will be lovers of themselves, lovers of money, self-assuming, haughty, blasphemers, disobedient to parents, unthankful, disloyal, having no natural affection, not open to any agreement, slanderers, without self-control, fierce, without love of goodness, betrayers, headstrong, puffed up with pride, lovers of pleasures rather than lovers of God, having a form of godly devotion but proving false to its power; and from these turn away.—2 Tim. 3:1-5.

Additional references: Matt. 24:4-14; Rev. 6:1-8; 12:1-12.

20. Who is Satan the Devil? Where did he and his demons come from?

Down the great dragon was hurled, the original serpent, the one called Devil and Satan, who is misleading the entire inhabited earth.—Rev. 12:9.

That one was a manslayer when he began, and he did not stand fast in the truth, because truth is not in him. When he speaks the lie, he speaks according to his own disposition, because he is a liar and the father of the lie.—John 8:44.

The angels that did not keep their original position but forsook their own proper dwelling place he has reserved with eternal bonds under dense darkness for the judgment of the great day.—Jude 6.

Additional references: Job 1:6; 2:1.

21. What challenge did Satan make against Jehovah and His rulership in the garden of Eden? What false accusation did Satan make against faithful Job?

Now the serpent . . . began to say to the woman: "Is it really so that God said you must not eat from every tree of the garden?" At this the woman said to the serpent: "Of the fruit of the trees of the garden we may eat. But as for eating of the fruit of the tree that is in the middle of the garden, God has said, 'You must not eat from it, no, you must not touch it that you do not die.'" At this the serpent said to the woman: "You positively will not die. For God knows that in the very day of your eating from it your eyes are bound to be opened and you are bound to be like God, knowing good and bad."—Gen. 3:1-5.

Satan answered Jehovah and said: "Is it for nothing that Job has feared God? Have not you yourself put up a hedge about him and about his house and about everything that he has all around? The work of his hands you have blessed, and his livestock itself has spread abroad in the earth. But, for a change, thrust out your hand, please, and touch everything he has and see whether he will not curse you to your very face."—Job 1:9-11.

Satan answered Jehovah and said: "Skin in behalf of skin, and everything that a man has he will give in behalf of his soul. For a change, thrust out your hand, please, and touch as far as his bone and his flesh and see whether he will not curse you to your very face."—Job 2:4, 5.

22. How can we personally show our support for Jehovah and his rulership and prove that Satan's accusations against God's servants are false?

Be wise, my son, and make my heart rejoice, that I may make a reply to him that is taunting me.—Prov. 27:11.

It is unthinkable on my part that I should declare you men righteous! Until I expire I shall not take away my integrity from myself!—Job 27:5.

Additional references: Ps. 26:11; Jas. 4:7.

23. What will become of Satan and his demons, according to Jehovah's judgment against them?

I shall put enmity between you and the woman and between your seed and her seed. He will bruise you in the head and you will bruise him in the heel.—Gen. 3:15.

For his part, the God who gives peace will crush Satan under your feet shortly. May the undeserved kindness of our Lord Jesus be with you.—Rom. 16:20.

I saw an angel coming down out of heaven with the key of the abyss and a great chain in his hand. And he seized the dragon, the original serpent, who is the Devil and Satan, and bound him for a thousand years.—Rev. 20:1, 2.

The Devil who was misleading them was hurled into the lake of fire and sulphur, where both the wild beast and the false prophet already were.—Rev. 20:10.

24. What are some of the spiritistic practices that Christians shun?

There should not be found in you anyone who makes his son or his daughter pass through the fire, anyone who employs divination, a practicer of magic or anyone who looks for omens or a sorcerer, or one who binds others with a spell or anyone who consults a spirit medium or a professional foreteller of events or anyone who inquires of the dead.—Deut. 18:10, 11.

As for the cowards and those without faith and those who are disgusting in their filth and murderers and fornicators and those practicing spiritism and idolaters and all the liars, their portion will be in the lake that burns with fire and sulphur. This means the second death.—Rev. 21:8.

25. What is the human soul? Can the soul die?

Jehovah God proceeded to form the man out of dust from the ground and to blow into his nostrils the breath of life, and the man came to be a living soul.—Gen. 2:7.

Look! All the souls—to me they belong. As the soul of the father so likewise the soul of the son—to me they belong. The soul that is sinning—it itself will die.—Ezek. 18:4.

26. What is sin? How did we all become sinners?

Everyone who practices sin is also practicing lawlessness, and so sin is lawlessness.—1 John 3:4.

Through one man sin entered into the world and death through sin, and thus death spread to all men because they had all sinned.—Rom. 5:12.

Additional reference: Ps. 51:5.

27. What should you do if you commit a serious sin?

My sin I finally confessed to you, and my error I did not cover. I said: "I shall make confession over my transgressions to Jehovah."—Ps. 32:5.

Is there anyone sick among you? Let him call the older men of the congregation to him, and let them pray over him, greasing him with oil in the name of Jehovah. And the prayer of faith will make the indisposed one well, and Jehovah will raise him up. Also, if he has committed sins, it will be forgiven him. Therefore openly confess your sins to one another and pray for one another, that you may get healed. A righteous man's supplication, when it is at work, has much force.—Jas. 5:14-16.

He that is covering over his transgressions will not succeed, but he that is confessing and leaving them will be shown mercy.—Prov. 28:13.

28. What should be our attitude toward sin?

Do not let sin continue to rule as king in your mortal bodies that you should obey their desires. Neither go on presenting your members to sin as weapons of unrighteousness, but present yourselves to God as those alive from the dead, also your members to God as weapons of righteousness. For sin must not be master over you, seeing that you are not under law but under undeserved kindness.—Rom. 6:12-14.

29. What is death?

In the sweat of your face you will eat bread until you return to the ground, for out of it you were taken. For dust you are and to dust you will return.—Gen. 3:19.

The living are conscious that they will die; but as for the dead, they are conscious of nothing at all, neither do they anymore have wages, because the remembrance of them has been forgotten.—Eccl. 9:5.

Additional references: Ps. 146:4; Eccl. 3:19, 20; 9:10; John 11:11-14.

30. Why do people die?

Through one man sin entered into the world and death through sin, and thus death spread to all men because they had all sinned.—Rom. 5:12.

The wages sin pays is death.—Rom. 6:23.

31. What hope is there for one who dies?

I have hope toward God, which hope these men themselves also entertain, that there is going to be a resurrection of both the righteous and the unrighteous.—Acts 24:15.

Do not marvel at this, because the hour is coming in which all those in the memorial tombs will hear his voice and come out, those who did good things to a resurrection of life, those who practiced vile things to a resurrection of judgment.—John 5:28, 29.

32. How many from among mankind will be raised to heavenly life with Jesus Christ?

I saw, and, look! the Lamb standing upon the Mount Zion, and with him a hundred and forty-four thousand having his name and the name of his Father written on their foreheads. And they are singing as if a new song before the throne and before the four living creatures and the elders; and no one was able to master that song but the hundred and forty-four thousand, who have been bought from the earth.—Rev. 14:1, 3.

33. What will those who are resurrected to heaven do there?

You made them to be a kingdom and priests to our God, and they are to rule as kings over the earth.—Rev. 5:10.

I saw thrones, and there were those who sat down on them, and power of judging was given them. . . . And they came to life and ruled as kings with the Christ for a thousand years. Happy and holy is anyone having part in the first resurrection; over these the second death has no authority, but they will be priests of God and of the Christ, and will rule as kings with him for the thousand years. —Rev. 20:4, 6.

34. What is the hope for mankind in general?

He went on to say: "Jesus, remember me when you get into your kingdom." And he said to him: "Truly I tell you today, You will be with me in Paradise."—Luke 23:42, 43.

I saw the dead, the great and the small, standing before the throne, and scrolls were opened. But another scroll was opened; it is the scroll of life. And the dead were judged out of those things written in the scrolls according to their deeds. And the sea gave up those dead in it, and death and Hades gave up those dead in them, and they were judged individually according to their deeds.—Rev. 20:12, 13.

Additional reference: Rev. 21:1-4.

35. Why should we hold firmly to our hope in the resurrection of the dead?

Do not become fearful of those who kill the body but cannot kill the soul; but rather be in fear of him that can destroy both soul and body in Gehenna.—Matt. 10:28.

PART II
JEHOVAH'S RIGHTEOUS REQUIREMENTS

In your study of the Bible, you have gained knowledge about what Jehovah expects of you and how to measure up to his righteous standards. Responding to what you learned may have entailed a number of adjustments in your attitude toward life itself and in your personal conduct. Now that you have resolved to live by Jehovah's standards of righteousness, you are in a position to render acceptable service as a minister of the good news.

A review of the following will help you fix clearly in mind Jehovah's righteous requirements and will remind you of some of the things you can do in order to become one of his approved servants. This information will impress upon you the importance of doing all things with a good conscience and to Jehovah's honor.—2 Cor. 1:12; 1 Tim. 1:19; 1 Pet. 3:16, 21.

1. What is the Christian standard for marriage?

In reply he said: "Did you not read that he who created them from the beginning made them male and female and said, 'For this reason a man will leave his father and his mother and will stick to his wife, and the two will be one flesh'? So that they are no longer two, but one flesh. Therefore, what God has yoked together let no man put apart." —Matt. 19:4-6.

The overseer should therefore be irreprehensible, a husband of one wife . . . Let ministerial servants be husbands of one wife.—1 Tim. 3:2, 12.

2. What is the only Scriptural basis for divorce that frees one to remarry?

I say to you that whoever divorces his wife, except on the ground of fornication, and marries another commits adultery.—Matt. 19:9.

3. What does the Bible say about married people separating from each other?

What God yoked together let no man put apart.—Mark 10:9.

To the married people I give instructions, yet not I but the Lord, that a wife should not depart from her husband; . . . and a husband should not leave his wife.—1 Cor. 7: 10, 11.

Additional reference: 1 Cor. 7:4, 5, 12-16.

4. Why should those living together as husband and wife be properly married?

Continue reminding them to be in subjection and be obedient to governments and authorities as rulers.—Titus 3:1.

Let marriage be honorable among all, and the marriage bed be without defilement, for God will judge fornicators and adulterers.—Heb. 13:4.

5. If you are married, are you sure that your marriage has been properly registered with the civil authorities?

For the Lord's sake subject yourselves to every human creation: whether to a king as being superior or to governors as being sent by him to inflict punishment on evildoers but to praise doers of good.—1 Pet. 2:13, 14.

6. Why should we show respect for the gift of life?

With you is the source of life; by light from you we can see light.—Ps. 36:9.

The God that made the world . . . gives to all persons life and breath and all things. For by him we have life and move and exist.—Acts 17:24, 25, 28.

Christ Jesus . . . gave himself a corresponding ransom for all.—1 Tim. 2:5, 6.

In case you build a new house, you must also make a parapet for your roof, that you may not place bloodguilt upon your house because someone falling might fall from it.—Deut. 22:8.

7. How does Jehovah view (a) the unlawful shedding of human blood? (b) abortion? (c) suicide?

As for the . . . murderers . . . , their portion will be in the lake that burns with fire and sulphur. This means the second death.—Rev. 21:8.

In case men should struggle with each other and they really hurt a pregnant woman and her children do come out but no fatal accident occurs, he is to have damages imposed . . . But if a fatal accident should occur, then you must give soul for soul.—Ex. 21:22, 23.

Look! All the souls—to me they belong. As the soul of the father so likewise the soul of the son—to me they belong.—Ezek. 18:4.

8. What responsibility rests upon a person who is infected with a communicable disease that is potentially fatal?

All things, therefore, that you want men to do to you, you also must likewise do to them; this, in fact, is what the Law and the Prophets mean.—Matt. 7:12.

Keeping an eye, not in personal interest upon just your own matters, but also in personal interest upon those of the others.—Phil. 2:4.

9. To avoid transmitting an infectious or a potentially fatal disease to others, why should an infected person (a) not initiate public displays of affection, such

as hugging and kissing? (b) attend the Congregation Book Study at the Kingdom Hall if at all possible? (c) not react negatively when some choose not to invite him into their homes? (d) Why should a person who may have been exposed to an infectious disease voluntarily choose to have a blood test before beginning a courtship? (e) Why should one having a communicable disease inform the presiding overseer before getting baptized?

Do not you people be owing anybody a single thing, except to love one another; for he that loves his fellowman has fulfilled the law. For the law code . . . is summed up in this word, namely, "You must love your neighbor as yourself." Love does not work evil to one's neighbor; therefore love is the law's fulfillment.—Rom. 13:8-10.

Love . . . does not behave indecently, does not look for its own interests, does not become provoked. It does not keep account of the injury.—1 Cor. 13:4, 5.

10. Why should Christians abstain from blood, and what does it mean to do so?

Only flesh with its soul—its blood—you must not eat. —Gen. 9:4.

Whenever your soul craves it you may slaughter, and you must eat meat according to the blessing of Jehovah your God . . . Only the blood you must not eat. On the earth you should pour it out as water.—Deut. 12:15, 16.

Keep abstaining from things sacrificed to idols and from blood and from things strangled.—Acts 15:29.

11. Are Christians under the Mosaic Law and its requirements regarding sacrifices and the Sabbath?

Christ is the end of the Law, so that everyone exercising faith may have righteousness.—Rom. 10:4.

Let no man judge you in eating and drinking or in respect of a festival or of an observance of the new moon or of a sabbath; for those things are a shadow of the things to come, but the reality belongs to the Christ.—Col. 2:16, 17.

Additional references: Gal. 3:24, 25; Col. 2:13, 14.

12. What Christian quality should outstandingly characterize our relationship with our spiritual brothers and sisters?

I am giving you a new commandment, that you love one another; just as I have loved you, that you also love one another. By this all will know that you are my disciples, if you have love among yourselves.—John 13:34, 35.

Clothe yourselves with love, for it is a perfect bond of union.—Col. 3:14.

Additional reference: 1 Cor. 13:4-7.

13. How should Christians view the shortcomings of fellow believers?

Continue putting up with one another and forgiving one another freely if anyone has a cause for complaint against another. Even as Jehovah freely forgave you, so do you also.—Col. 3:13.

Above all things, have intense love for one another, because love covers a multitude of sins.—1 Pet. 4:8.

Additional references: Prov. 17:9; 19:11; Matt. 7:1-5.

14. If your brother's sin against you is of a serious nature, what should you do?

If your brother commits a sin, go lay bare his fault between you and him alone. If he listens to you, you have gained your brother. But if he does not listen, take along with you one or two more, in order that at the mouth of two or three witnesses every matter may be established. If he does not listen to them, speak to the congregation. If he does not listen even to the congregation, let him be to you just as a man of the nations and as a tax collector.—Matt. 18:15-17.

15. What is the fruitage of the spirit, and how will cultivating it help us to maintain a fine relationship with others?

The fruitage of the spirit is love, joy, peace, longsuffering, kindness, goodness, faith, mildness, self-control.—Gal. 5:22, 23.

16. Why must lying be avoided?

The Devil . . . did not stand fast in the truth, because truth is not in him. When he speaks the lie, he speaks according to his own disposition, because he is a liar and the father of the lie.—John 8:44.

As for . . . all the liars, their portion will be in the lake that burns with fire and sulphur.—Rev. 21:8.

Additional references: Ex. 20:16; 2 Cor. 6:4, 7.

17. What is the Christian view of stealing?

Let none of you suffer as a murderer or a thief.—1 Pet. 4:15.

Let the stealer steal no more, but rather let him do hard work, doing with his hands what is good work, that he may have something to distribute to someone in need.—Eph. 4:28.

18. Does the Bible prohibit the use of alcoholic beverages in moderation?

Go, eat your food with rejoicing and drink your wine with a good heart, because already the true God has found pleasure in your works.—Eccl. 9:7.

Do not drink water any longer, but use a little wine for the sake of your stomach and your frequent cases of sickness.—1 Tim. 5:23.

19. What is the Christian view of overdrinking and drunkenness?

What! Do you not know that unrighteous persons will not inherit God's kingdom? Do not be misled. Neither fornicators, nor idolaters, nor adulterers, . . . nor greedy persons, nor drunkards . . . will inherit God's kingdom. —1 Cor. 6:9, 10.

Do not come to be among heavy drinkers of wine. —Prov. 23:20.

The overseer should therefore be irreprehensible, . . . not a drunken brawler.—1 Tim. 3:2, 3.

Ministerial servants should likewise be serious, . . . not giving themselves to a lot of wine.—1 Tim. 3:8.

Additional references: 1 Cor. 5:11; 1 Pet. 4:3.

20. Why should Christians abstain from all nonmedical use of addictive or mind-altering natural or synthetic substances?

I entreat you by the compassions of God, brothers, to present your bodies a sacrifice living, holy, acceptable to God, a sacred service with your power of reason. And quit being fashioned after this system of things, but be transformed by making your mind over, that you may prove to yourselves the good and acceptable and perfect will of God.—Rom. 12:1, 2.

Let us cleanse ourselves of every defilement of flesh and spirit, perfecting holiness in God's fear.—2 Cor. 7:1.

Additional references: 1 Pet. 4:7; Rev. 21:8, *Int.*

21. What does the Bible say about fornication, which includes adultery, sexual relations with another person of the same sex, and other ungodly sexual conduct?

Now the works of the flesh are manifest, and they are fornication, uncleanness, loose conduct, . . . and things like these. . . . Those who practice such things will not inherit God's kingdom.—Gal. 5:19-21.

What! Do you not know that unrighteous persons will not inherit God's kingdom? Do not be misled. Neither fornicators, nor idolaters, nor adulterers, nor men kept for unnatural purposes, nor men who lie with men . . . will inherit God's kingdom.—1 Cor. 6:9, 10.

God gave them up to disgraceful sexual appetites, for both their females changed the natural use of themselves into one contrary to nature; and likewise even the males left the natural use of the female and became violently inflamed in their lust toward one another, males with males, working what is obscene and receiving in themselves the full recompense, which was due for their error.—Rom. 1: 26, 27.

Let marriage be honorable among all, and the marriage bed be without defilement, for God will judge fornicators and adulterers.—Heb. 13:4.

Additional references: Mark 7:20-23; Eph. 5:5; 1 Pet. 4:3; Rev. 21:8.

22. By adhering to what Bible counsel will you be able to resist temptations and pressures that could induce you to engage in sexual immorality?

Keep your minds fixed on the things above, not on the things upon the earth. Deaden, therefore, your body members that are upon the earth as respects fornication, uncleanness, sexual appetite, hurtful desire, and covetousness, which is idolatry.—Col. 3:2, 5.

Brothers, whatever things are true, whatever things are of serious concern, whatever things are righteous, whatever things are chaste, whatever things are lovable, whatever things are well spoken of, whatever virtue there is and whatever praiseworthy thing there is, continue considering these things.—Phil. 4:8.

23. Why must a Christian avoid becoming involved in any form of gambling?

You men are those leaving Jehovah, those forgetting my holy mountain, those setting in order a table for the god of Good Luck and those filling up mixed wine for the god of Destiny.—Isa. 65:11.

Do you not know that unrighteous persons will not inherit God's kingdom? Do not be misled. Neither . . . thieves, nor greedy persons . . . will inherit God's kingdom. —1 Cor. 6:9, 10.

24. If a person commits a serious sin out of weakness but wants help to be restored to Jehovah's favor, what action should he take immediately?

My sin I finally confessed to you, and my error I did not cover. I said: "I shall make confession over my transgressions to Jehovah."—Ps. 32:5.

Is there anyone suffering evil among you? Let him carry on prayer. Is there anyone in good spirits? Let him sing psalms. Is there anyone sick among you? Let him call the older men of the congregation to him, and let them pray over him, greasing him with oil in the name of Jehovah. And the prayer of faith will make the indisposed one well, and Jehovah will raise him up. Also, if he has committed sins, it will be forgiven him.—Jas. 5:13-15.

Additional references: Prov. 28:13; 1 John 2:1, 2.

25. In addition to confessing his own sins, each Christian has what responsibility regarding serious wrongdoing by others that could threaten the spiritual or moral cleanness of the congregation?

In case a soul sins in that he has heard public cursing and he is a witness or he has seen it or has come to know of it, if he does not report it, then he must answer for his error. —Lev. 5:1.

26. What is the proper viewpoint to have if one is Scripturally reproved?

The discipline of Jehovah, O my son, do not reject; and do not abhor his reproof.—Prov. 3:11.

The commandment is a lamp, and a light the law is, and the reproofs of discipline are the way of life.—Prov. 6:23.

27. What action does the congregation take when a person in its midst proves to be an unrepentant violator of God's commandments?

In my letter I wrote you to quit mixing in company with fornicators, not meaning entirely with the fornicators of this world or the greedy persons and extortioners or idolaters. Otherwise, you would actually have to get out of the world. But now I am writing you to quit mixing in company with anyone called a brother that is a fornicator or a greedy person or an idolater or a reviler or a drunkard or an extortioner, not even eating with such a man. For what do I have to do with judging those outside? Do you not judge those inside, while God judges those outside? "Remove the wicked man from among yourselves."—1 Cor. 5: 9-13.

28. What is idolatry? What are some forms of idolatry that Christians must guard against today?

You must not make for yourself a carved image or a form like anything that is in the heavens above or that is on the earth underneath or that is in the waters under the earth. You must not bow down to them nor be induced to serve them, because I Jehovah your God am a God exacting exclusive devotion.—Ex. 20:4, 5.

Guard yourselves from idols.—1 John 5:21.

Additional references: Isa. 42:8; Jer. 10:14, 15.

29. What is the Christian's position as to the world alienated from God?

They are no part of the world, just as I am no part of the world.—John 17:16.

Do you not know that the friendship with the world is enmity with God? Whoever, therefore, wants to be a friend of the world is constituting himself an enemy of God. —Jas. 4:4.

30. What was Jesus' attitude toward participation in the political affairs of the world?

The Devil took him along to an unusually high mountain, and showed him all the kingdoms of the world and their glory, and he said to him: "All these things I will give you if you fall down and do an act of worship to me." Then Jesus said to him: "Go away, Satan! For it is written, 'It is Jehovah your God you must worship, and it is to him alone you must render sacred service.'"—Matt. 4:8-10.

Jesus, knowing they were about to come and seize him to make him king, withdrew again into the mountain all alone.—John 6:15.

31. When a person separates himself from the world and becomes a Christian, what treatment should he expect from those in the world?

If you were part of the world, the world would be fond of what is its own. Now because you are no part of the world, but I have chosen you out of the world, on this account the world hates you. . . . If they have persecuted me, they will persecute you also.—John 15:19, 20.

All those desiring to live with godly devotion in association with Christ Jesus will also be persecuted.—2 Tim. 3:12.

Because you do not continue running with them in this course to the same low sink of debauchery, they are puzzled and go on speaking abusively of you.—1 Pet. 4:4.

32. How does being separate from the world affect a Christian in his choice of secular employment?

Let the stealer steal no more, but rather let him do hard work, doing with his hands what is good work, that he may have something to distribute to someone in need.—Eph. 4:28.

The Devil . . . is a liar and the father of the lie.—John 8:44.

He will certainly render judgment among many peoples, and set matters straight respecting mighty nations far away. And they will have to beat their swords into plowshares and their spears into pruning shears. They will not lift up sword, nation against nation, neither will they learn war anymore.—Mic. 4:3.

I heard another voice out of heaven say: "Get out of her [Babylon the Great], my people, if you do not want to share with her in her sins, and if you do not want to receive part of her plagues."—Rev. 18:4.

33. What Bible principles should a Christian apply regarding his choice of entertainment and recreation?

Do not be misled. Bad associations spoil useful habits. —1 Cor. 15:33.

Brothers, whatever things are true, whatever things are of serious concern, whatever things are righteous, whatever things are chaste, whatever things are lovable, whatever things are well spoken of, whatever virtue there is and whatever praiseworthy thing there is, continue considering these things.—Phil. 4:8.

Do not be loving either the world or the things in the world.—1 John 2:15.

Keep strict watch that how you walk is not as unwise but as wise persons, buying out the opportune time for yourselves, because the days are wicked. On this account cease becoming unreasonable, but go on perceiving what the will of Jehovah is. Also, do not be getting drunk with wine, in which there is debauchery, but keep getting filled with spirit, speaking to yourselves with psalms and praises to God and spiritual songs, singing and accompanying yourselves with music in your hearts to Jehovah, in the name of our Lord Jesus Christ giving thanks always for all things to our God and Father.—Eph. 5:15-20.

Let fornication and uncleanness of every sort or greediness not even be mentioned among you, just as it befits holy people.—Eph. 5:3.

34. Would it be proper for true Christians to share in worship with other religious groups?

I heard another voice out of heaven say: "Get out of her [Babylon the Great], my people, if you do not want to share with her in her sins, and if you do not want to receive part of her plagues. For her sins have massed together clear up to heaven, and God has called her acts of injustice to mind."—Rev. 18:4, 5.

Additional references: Matt. 7:13, 14, 21-23; 1 Cor. 10:20; 2 Cor. 6:14-18.

35. What is the only religious ceremony that Christians are commanded to observe?

He took a loaf, gave thanks, broke it, and gave it to them, saying: "This means my body which is to be given in your behalf. Keep doing this in remembrance of me."—Luke 22:19.

Additional reference: 1 Cor. 11:23-26.

36. How can you determine whether you should observe or participate in celebrations that are popular in your community?

They are no part of the world, just as I am no part of the world.—John 17:16.

You cannot be partaking of "the table of Jehovah" and the table of demons.—1 Cor. 10:21.

They went mingling with the nations and took up learning their works.—Ps. 106:35.

The time that has passed by is sufficient for you to have worked out the will of the nations when you proceeded in deeds of loose conduct, lusts, excesses with wine, revelries, drinking matches, and illegal idolatries.—1 Pet. 4:3.

37. What birthday celebrations are mentioned in the Bible? How does this affect your view of birthday celebrations?

When Herod's birthday was being celebrated the daughter of Herodias danced at it and pleased Herod so much that he promised with an oath to give her whatever she asked. Then she, under her mother's coaching, said: "Give me here upon a platter the head of John the Baptist." Grieved though he was, the king out of regard for his oaths and for those reclining with him commanded it to be given; and he sent and had John beheaded in the prison. And his head was brought on a platter and given to the maiden, and she brought it to her mother.—Matt. 14:6-11.

Additional references: Gen. 40:20-22; Eccl. 7:1, 8.

PART III
JEHOVAH'S ARRANGEMENT OF THINGS

Through your study of the Bible, you have learned that Jehovah has a purpose to bring all things back into subjection to himself, just as they were in the beginning. (1 Cor. 15:24-28; Eph. 1:8-10) Having reached this point in your study, you are no doubt eager to find your place in Jehovah's arrangement and to be submissive to his rule. The following questions and Scripture references will help you examine your own understanding of submission to Jehovah's arrangements regarding congregation organization, Christian family life, and the political elements of this system of things. You will be able to examine your appreciation for Jehovah's arrangement for educating and building up his people spiritually. That includes your attending and participating in congregation meetings to the extent of your circumstances and ability.

Additionally, this section will focus on the importance of having a regular share in the Kingdom-preaching work, helping others to come to know Jehovah and what he is doing for mankind. (Matt. 24:14; 28:19, 20) Finally, it will impress upon your mind the seriousness of dedicating yourself to Jehovah God before submitting to water baptism. You can be certain that Jehovah appreciates your sincere response to his undeserved kindness expressed in your behalf.

1. In God's arrangement of things, who is the head of the married woman?

You wives, be in subjection to your husbands, as it is becoming in the Lord.—Col. 3:18.

Let wives be in subjection to their husbands as to the Lord, because a husband is head of his wife as the Christ also is head of the congregation, he being a savior of this body.—Eph. 5:22, 23.

2. How should a husband exercise headship over his wife?

Husbands ought to be loving their wives as their own bodies. He who loves his wife loves himself, for no man ever hated his own flesh; but he feeds and cherishes it, as the Christ also does the congregation.—Eph. 5:28, 29.

You husbands, keep on loving your wives and do not be bitterly angry with them.—Col. 3:19.

3. Is the wife whose husband is not a believer freed from his headship?

You wives, be in subjection to your own husbands, in order that, if any are not obedient to the word, they may be won without a word through the conduct of their wives, because of having been eyewitnesses of your chaste conduct together with deep respect.—1 Pet. 3:1, 2.

4. Who is primarily responsible before God for the training and disciplining of children?

Fathers, do not be irritating your children, but go on bringing them up in the discipline and mental-regulating of Jehovah.—Eph. 6:4.

5. What responsibility do children have in the family arrangement?

Children, be obedient to your parents in union with the Lord, for this is righteous: "Honor your father and your mother"; which is the first command with a promise: "That it may go well with you and you may endure a long time on the earth."—Eph. 6:1-3.

You children, be obedient to your parents in everything, for this is well-pleasing in the Lord.—Col. 3:20.

6. What is the proper attitude for Christians to maintain toward worldly rulers?

Let every soul be in subjection to the superior authorities, for there is no authority except by God; the existing authorities stand placed in their relative positions by God. —Rom. 13:1.

Continue reminding them to be in subjection and be obedient to governments and authorities as rulers.—Titus 3:1.

7. Must a Christian pay all taxes and assessments demanded by law?

Render to all their dues, to him who calls for the tax, the tax; to him who calls for the tribute, the tribute; to him who calls for fear, such fear; to him who calls for honor, such honor.—Rom. 13:7.

Additional reference: Luke 20:21-25.

8. Are there any circumstances under which a Christian would refuse to obey worldly rulers?

With that they called them and charged them, nowhere to make any utterance or to teach upon the basis of the name of Jesus. But in reply Peter and John said to them: "Whether it is righteous in the sight of God to listen to you rather than to God, judge for yourselves. But as for us, we cannot stop speaking about the things we have seen and heard."—Acts 4:18-20.

In answer Peter and the other apostles said: "We must obey God as ruler rather than men."—Acts 5:29.

9. Should Christians comply with legal requirements that do not conflict with God's laws, such as registering marriages and births, responding to census inquiries, or obtaining required licenses and permits?

In those days a decree went forth . . . for all the inhabited earth to be registered . . . Of course, Joseph also went up from Galilee . . . to get registered with Mary, who had been given him in marriage.—Luke 2:1-5.

Continue reminding them to be in subjection and be obedient to governments and authorities as rulers.—Titus 3:1.

10. What is the headship arrangement in the Christian congregation?

I want you to know that the head of every man is the Christ; in turn the head of a woman is the man; in turn the head of the Christ is God.—1 Cor. 11:3.

11. Who is the Head of the Christian congregation?

He is the image of the invisible God, the firstborn of all creation; because by means of him all other things were created in the heavens and upon the earth, the things visible and the things invisible, no matter whether they are thrones or lordships or governments or authorities. All other things have been created through him and for him. Also, he is before all other things and by means of him all other things were made to exist, and he is the head of the body, the congregation.—Col. 1:15-18.

12. How can you identify "the faithful and discreet slave" today?

Who really is the faithful and discreet slave whom his master appointed over his domestics, to give them their food at the proper time? Happy is that slave if his master on arriving finds him doing so. Truly I say to you, He will appoint him over all his belongings.—Matt. 24:45-47.

13. What is the Governing Body of the Christian congregation?

Certain men came down from Judea and began to teach the brothers: "Unless you get circumcised according to the custom of Moses, you cannot be saved." But when there had occurred no little dissension and disputing by Paul and Barnabas with them, they arranged for Paul and Barnabas and some others of them to go up to the apostles and older men in Jerusalem regarding this dispute.—Acts 15:1, 2.

As they traveled on through the cities they would deliver to those there for observance the decrees that had been decided upon by the apostles and older men who were in Jerusalem. Therefore, indeed, the congregations continued to be made firm in the faith and to increase in number from day to day.—Acts 16:4, 5.

14. By what visible means is Christ's headship represented in the congregation?

Pay attention to yourselves and to all the flock, among which the holy spirit has appointed you overseers, to shepherd the congregation of God, which he purchased with the blood of his own Son.—Acts 20:28.

To the older men among you I give this exhortation . . . Shepherd the flock of God in your care, not under compulsion, but willingly; neither for love of dishonest gain, but eagerly; neither as lording it over those who are God's inheritance, but becoming examples to the flock.—1 Pet. 5:1-3.

15. How do members of the congregation demonstrate submission to the headship of Christ in the congregation?

Remember those who are taking the lead among you, who have spoken the word of God to you, and as you contemplate how their conduct turns out imitate their faith. —Heb. 13:7.

Be obedient to those who are taking the lead among you and be submissive, for they are keeping watch over your souls as those who will render an account; that they may do this with joy and not with sighing, for this would be damaging to you.—Heb. 13:17.

16. Whose ideas are recorded in the Bible? Why should you regularly study God's Word?

All Scripture is inspired of God and beneficial for teaching, for reproving, for setting things straight, for disciplining in righteousness, that the man of God may be fully competent, completely equipped for every good work. —2 Tim. 3:16, 17.

His delight is in the law of Jehovah, and in his law he reads in an undertone day and night. And he will certainly become like a tree planted by streams of water, that gives its own fruit in its season and the foliage of which does not wither, and everything he does will succeed.—Ps. 1:2, 3.

Additional references: Deut. 17:18-20; Prov. 2:1-6.

17. Why is it beneficial to attend the meetings arranged by the congregation? What efforts do you make to do so?

My own foot will certainly stand on a level place; among the congregated throngs I shall bless Jehovah.—Ps. 26:12.

Let us consider one another to incite to love and fine works, not forsaking the gathering of ourselves together, as some have the custom, but encouraging one another, and all the more so as you behold the day drawing near. —Heb. 10:24, 25.

18. Why should you participate in congregation meetings as your circumstances allow?

I will declare your name to my brothers; in the middle of the congregation I shall praise you.—Ps. 22:22.

By iron, iron itself is sharpened. So one man sharpens the face of another.—Prov. 27:17.

Let us always offer to God a sacrifice of praise, that is, the fruit of lips which make public declaration to his name.—Heb. 13:15.

19. Why must approved works accompany our Christian faith?

Faith, if it does not have works, is dead in itself. Nevertheless, a certain one will say: "You have faith, and I have works. Show me your faith apart from the works, and I shall show you my faith by my works." Indeed, as the body without spirit is dead, so also faith without works is dead. —Jas. 2:17, 18, 26.

20. What urgent work does the Bible set out for all Christians?

This good news of the kingdom will be preached in all the inhabited earth for a witness to all the nations; and then the end will come.—Matt. 24:14.

Go therefore and make disciples of people of all the nations, baptizing them in the name of the Father and of the Son and of the holy spirit, teaching them to observe all the things I have commanded you.—Matt. 28:19, 20.

21. Are you sharing the good news of the Kingdom with others? In what ways?

I did not hold back from telling you any of the things that were profitable nor from teaching you publicly and from house to house. But I thoroughly bore witness both to Jews and to Greeks about repentance toward God and faith in our Lord Jesus.—Acts 20:20, 21.

He began to reason . . . in the marketplace with those who happened to be on hand.—Acts 17:17.

22. Why should you take seriously your responsibility to share the good news with others?

I call you to witness this very day that I am clean from the blood of all men, for I have not held back from telling you all the counsel of God.—Acts 20:26, 27.

If, now, I am declaring the good news, it is no reason for me to boast, for necessity is laid upon me. Really, woe is me if I did not declare the good news!—1 Cor. 9:16.

23. How can we give material support to the Kingdom work today?

Honor Jehovah with your valuable things and with the firstfruits of all your produce. Then your stores of supply will be filled with plenty; and with new wine your own press vats will overflow.—Prov. 3:9, 10.

24. How can we demonstrate our love for brothers and sisters who come to be in need of material assistance?

If a brother or a sister is in a naked state and lacking the food sufficient for the day, yet a certain one of you says to them: "Go in peace, keep warm and well fed," but you do not give them the necessities for their body, of what benefit is it?—Jas. 2:15, 16.

Additional references: Prov. 3:27; Jas. 1:27.

25. What should be our attitude toward giving of ourselves and of our material possessions in Jehovah's service?

Who am I and who are my people, that we should retain power to make voluntary offerings like this? For everything is from you, and out of your own hand we have given to you.—1 Chron. 29:14.

Let each one do just as he has resolved in his heart, not grudgingly or under compulsion, for God loves a cheerful giver.—2 Cor. 9:7.

26. What attitude should we have when we are persecuted or undergoing trial?

Happy are those who have been persecuted for righteousness' sake, since the kingdom of the heavens belongs to them. Happy are you when people reproach you and persecute you and lyingly say every sort of wicked thing against you for my sake. Rejoice and leap for joy, since your reward is great in the heavens; for in that way they persecuted the prophets prior to you.—Matt. 5:10-12.

Consider it all joy, my brothers, when you meet with various trials, knowing as you do that this tested quality of your faith works out endurance.—Jas. 1:2, 3.

These, therefore, went their way from before the Sanhedrin, rejoicing because they had been counted worthy to be dishonored in behalf of his name.—Acts 5:41.

27. To whom and in whose name should we pray?

O Hearer of prayer, even to you people of all flesh will come.—Ps. 65:2.

In that day you will ask me no question at all. Most truly I say to you, If you ask the Father for anything he will give it to you in my name.—John 16:23.

Additional reference: John 14:6.

28. How should we pray so as to be heard by Jehovah?

When you pray, you must not be as the hypocrites; because they like to pray standing in the synagogues and on the corners of the broad ways to be visible to men. Truly I say to you, They are having their reward in full. You, however, when you pray, go into your private room and, after shutting your door, pray to your Father who is in secret; then your Father who looks on in secret will repay you. But when praying, do not say the same things over and over again, just as the people of the nations do, for they imagine they will get a hearing for their use of many words. So, do not make yourselves like them, for God your Father knows what things you are needing before ever you ask him.—Matt. 6:5-8.

29. What are some of the things you can pray about?

You must pray, then, this way: "Our Father in the heavens, let your name be sanctified. Let your kingdom come. Let your will take place, as in heaven, also upon earth. Give us today our bread for this day; and forgive us our debts, as we also have forgiven our debtors. And do not bring us into temptation, but deliver us from the wicked one."—Matt. 6:9-13.

This is the confidence that we have toward him, that, no matter what it is that we ask according to his will, he hears us.—1 John 5:14.

30. What effect might our conduct have on our prayers?

You husbands, continue dwelling in like manner with them according to knowledge, assigning them honor as to a weaker vessel, the feminine one, since you are also heirs with them of the undeserved favor of life, in order for your prayers not to be hindered. For the eyes of Jehovah are upon the righteous ones, and his ears are toward their supplication; but the face of Jehovah is against those doing bad things.—1 Pet. 3:7, 12.

Additional reference: Isa. 1:15-17.

31. Why do Jehovah's Witnesses baptize in water those who embrace the Christian faith?

Go therefore and make disciples of people of all the nations, baptizing them in the name of the Father and of the Son and of the holy spirit.—Matt. 28:19.

In the course of those days Jesus came from Nazareth of Galilee and was baptized in the Jordan by John.—Mark 1:9.

32. Why is it appropriate for dedicated and baptized Christians to be called Jehovah's Witnesses?

"You are my witnesses," is the utterance of Jehovah, "even my servant whom I have chosen, in order that you may know and have faith in me, and that you may understand that I am the same One. Before me there was no God formed, and after me there continued to be none. I—I am Jehovah, and besides me there is no savior. I myself have told forth and have saved and have caused it to be heard, when there was among you no strange god. So you are my witnesses," is the utterance of Jehovah, "and I am God." —Isa. 43:10-12.

CONCLUDING DISCUSSION WITH BAPTISM CANDIDATES

Baptisms are usually performed at assemblies and conventions of Jehovah's Witnesses. At the conclusion of the baptism talk, the speaker will ask the baptism candidates to stand and answer the following two questions in a loud, clear voice:

On the basis of the sacrifice of Jesus Christ, have you repented of your sins and dedicated yourself to Jehovah to do his will?

Do you understand that your dedication and baptism identify you as one of Jehovah's Witnesses in association with God's spirit-directed organization?

Affirmative answers to these questions constitute a "public declaration" of the baptism candidates' faith in the ransom and of the fact that they have unreservedly dedicated themselves to Jehovah. (Rom. 10:9, 10) Baptism candidates will therefore want to give prayerful advance thought to these questions so that they can answer in harmony with their personal convictions.

• **What is appropriate attire for baptism?** (John 15:19; Phil. 1:10; 1 Tim. 2:9)

Those being baptized will want to wear modest clothing, keeping in mind the importance of the occasion. Thus, a swimsuit that is immodest would be unbecoming attire for a Christian and should be avoided. Likewise, it would be inappropriate for one to be unkempt or slovenly in appearance. Further, it would be fitting to avoid wearing garments with worldly sayings or commercial slogans. In this way, the dignity of the occasion will be maintained, and we will continue to stand out as different from the world.

• **How should a person conduct himself when getting baptized?** (Luke 3:21, 22)

Jesus' baptism set the example for Christian baptisms today. He appreciated that baptism is a serious step, and this was reflected in his attitude and actions. Hence, the baptism site would not be the place for jesting, swimming, or other conduct that would detract from the seriousness of the occasion. Neither would a new Christian carry on as though he had won a great victory. While baptism is a joyful occasion, that joy should be expressed in a dignified manner.

• **Even after you are baptized, why will it be vital for you to maintain a good schedule of personal study and to share regularly in the ministry?**

• **How will staying in close association with the congregation help you to carry out your dedication to Jehovah?**

• **Are you now thoroughly convinced that you should be baptized at the first opportunity?**

INSTRUCTIONS FOR CONGREGATION ELDERS

When an unbaptized publisher makes known to the elders his desire to be baptized, he should be encouraged to review carefully the "Questions for Those Desiring to Be Baptized," found on pages 182-215. His attention should be directed to "A Message to the Unbaptized Publisher," beginning on page 180, which explains how he can prepare for the discussions with the elders. As noted there, the prospective baptism candidate may use his personal notes made on a separate sheet of paper and may have this book open during the discussions. However, there is no need for someone to go over the questions with the person before he meets with the elders.

The presiding overseer should be informed of the person's desire to be baptized. After the person requesting baptism has had time to review the information, the presiding overseer will make arrangements for some of the elders to have discussions with the person based on that material. It is not necessary to wait until an assembly is announced before having these discussions. The three parts can usually be covered in three sessions of about one hour each, although there is no objection to using more time if that is necessary. Neither the candidate nor the elder should be rushed in going through the questions. Where possible, a different elder should be assigned to handle each of the sessions. It would be good to open and close each session with prayer.

Usually it is best to review the questions with each baptism candidate individually, not in a group. By having each candidate comment on every question, the elders will get a clear picture of his depth of understanding, leaving no doubt as to whether he is ready for baptism or not. Additionally, the one requesting baptism may be more inclined to express himself in this setting. A husband and wife may be interviewed together. When the baptism candidate is a sister, the discussions should be held in such a way that the elder is never alone with her.

On occasion, there may be a circumstance in which it is appropriate to meet with more than one candidate at a time. It may be practical to meet with a husband and wife or other family members as a group, especially if they have studied together and plan to be baptized at the same time. Or if there are few elders and many preparing for baptism, it may be necessary to meet with the candidates in groups of not more than two or three. The elders should exercise good judgment in making such arrangements.

The elders will make sure that a person to be baptized has acquired a *reasonable* understanding of basic Bible teachings. Additionally, they will want to ascertain whether the prospective minister deeply appreciates the truth and demonstrates proper respect for Jehovah's organization. If the person does not understand primary Bible teachings, the elders will arrange for him to receive the necessary personal assistance so as to qualify for baptism at a later time. Others may need to be given time to demonstrate more appreciation for field service or submissiveness to organizational arrangements. It will be up to the elders to use discretion in apportioning the hour or so spent in each session so as to discern fully whether the baptism candidate is ready to take this important step. Although more time may be spent on certain questions and less on others, *all* the questions should be reviewed.

The elders assigned to help a baptism candidate will meet after the third session and decide whether the person should be accepted for baptism or not. Elders will take into consideration the background, ability, and other circumstances of each baptism candidate. Our interest is in those who have turned their hearts to Jehovah and who have grasped the sense of fundamental Bible truths. With your loving assistance, those being baptized will be helped to enter into the Christian ministry adequately prepared to accomplish that important assignment.

Thereafter, one or two of the assigned elders should meet with the person and inform him whether he qualifies for baptism or not. If the person qualifies, the elders should review with him the "Concluding Discussion With Baptism Candidates," found on pages 215-16. This discussion need take only ten minutes or less.

SUBJECT INDEX